ONE EARTH

Anuradha Rao

People
of Color
Protecting
Our Planet

ORCA BOOK PUBLISHERS

Published in Canada and the United States in 2020 by Orca Book Publishers.
orcabook.com

Library and Archives Canada Cataloguing in Publication
Title: One Earth: people of color protecting our planet / Anuradha Rao.
Names: Rao, Anuradha S., 1975– author.
Description: Includes bibliographical references and index.
Identifiers: Canadiana (print) 20190177551 | Canadiana (ebook) 20190177616 |
ISBN 9781459818866 (softcover) | ISBN 9781459818873 (PDF) | ISBN 9781459818880 (EPUB)
Subjects: LCSH: Environmentalists—Biography—Juvenile literature. | LCSH: Conservationists—Biography—
Juvenile literature. | LCSH: Environmentalism—Juvenile literature. | LCSH: Environmental protection—
Juvenile literature. | LCSH: Minorities—Political activity—Juvenile literature.
Classification: LCC GE195.5 .R36 2020 | DDC j333.72092—dc23

Library of Congress Control Number: 2019947360

Summary: This nonfiction book for teens profiles 20 environmental defenders
of color from around the world. Their individual stories show that the intersection
of environment and ethnicity is an asset to protecting our planet.
Illustrated with photos of each of the people profiled.

Orca Book Publishers is committed to reducing the consumption of nonrenewable resources in the making of our books. We make every effort to use materials that support a sustainable future.

Orca Book Publishers gratefully acknowledges the support for its publishing programs provided by the following agencies: the Government of Canada, the Canada Council for the Arts and the Province of British Columbia through the BC Arts Council and the Book Publishing Tax Credit.

Edited by Sarah N. Harvey
Design by Rachel Page

Cover illustration by kotoffei/creativemarket.com. Cover photos courtesy of Efe Peker,
Michael Ruffolo, Joanna Marquis, John Nation, Ghanimat Azhdari, Brandon Nguyen,
The Arctic Eider Society, Danielle Stark, Dipani Sutaria, Dr. Clotilda Yakimchuk

Printed and bound in South Korea.

24 23 22 21 • 3 4 5 6

To Leela: past, present and future

CONTENTS

INTRODUCTION

Who is an environmental defender? What does she, he or they look like? Maybe like you. Maybe like me.

I've worked and volunteered in the environmental field since the 1990s. But I've often felt like the odd one out. Only one other person in my family has gone into this line of work. And at work, I've usually been the only one with a brown face. It makes me feel a bit weird. I don't have the same traditions or listen to the same kind of music as my colleagues. I celebrate different holidays. I was born in Canada, but my mother tongue isn't English and no one can pronounce my name.

My ancestors fled environmental crisis in the north of India more than 2,000 years ago and religious persecution in Goa 500 years ago. My grandfather was a freedom fighter against a colonial system imposed on India. That history shapes me and makes me different from most of the people I have worked with. I can move fluidly between both worlds—family and work—but I end up hiding a bit of my true self from almost everyone. I know I have one identity, not two—my culture and my passion for the earth are linked.

Being different isn't bad though. Because I navigate between cultures every day, it's easy for me to be a bridge between groups of people who wouldn't otherwise talk to each other.

Very few people of color are seen to be at the forefront of the environmental movement. David Suzuki, Vandana Shiva and Wangari Maathai are notable exceptions. Others exist in places where we tend not to look. They save animals, stop destruction, research solutions, fight for health and justice, and do many other brave things. Some risk their lives defending nature.

When I was looking for people to interview for this book, I found more than I could possibly include. I could have written an entire book about environmental defenders of color in Vancouver, British Columbia, where I live, or a whole book about **Indigenous** protectors of culture, land and water. But one goal of this book is to showcase diversity—in background, location, age and interest. The people in this book don't represent all the people from their nations, ethnicities or cultures. They spoke to me about themselves, their own experiences, and events as they recalled them.

I chose to focus on 20 environmental defenders. You'll learn about what they're defending and how. You'll see how their cultures and backgrounds influence their work. And you'll hear the words and wisdom they've shared to inspire you. They're the role models I wish I'd had when I was younger.

LINDA MUELLER

MY INSPIRATIONS

Dr. Mao Amis (Uganda/South Africa) founded the African Centre for a Green Economy to provide thought leadership and showcase local solutions to environmental challenges.
IMAGE CREDIT: NONCEBA AMIS

Kim Sander Wright (Canada) felt the environmental movement didn't appreciate the approaches of people from different cultures, so she decided to work with people who see things holistically, as her culture had taught her to.
IMAGE CREDIT: KIM SANDER WRIGHT

Arun and Poornima Venkataramanan (India) have been running a sea turtle conservation program with students for more than two decades. They started Marudam Farm School to combine education, ecosystem restoration, organic farming and poverty reduction.
IMAGE CREDIT: ARUN VENKATARAMANAN

The David Suzuki Foundation's Sustainable Diversity Network (Canada) celebrates environmental voices and stories that are often unheard or unacknowledged.
IMAGE CREDIT: DAVID SUZUKI FOUNDATION

The Tsleil-Waututh Nation is a leader in research, restoration and protection of their traditional and ***unceded*** lands and waters, which include what is now Canada's third-largest city, Vancouver.
IMAGE CREDIT: AARON BLAKE EVANS

OUTDOOR AFRO

One

GETTING PEOPLE INVOLVED

Gathering
Young Voices

BRANDON NGUYEN

Co-founder, Toronto Coalition of EcoSchools
Born in Toronto, Ontario; lives in Philadelphia, Pennsylvania

I see myself as a young Vietnamese-Canadian.

W ho knew that watching *Animal Planet* could help you start your own nonprofit organization? Brandon Nguyen laughs when he thinks about his earliest environmental inspirations, which included that television channel as well as keeping frogs and lizards as pets.

"I was really lucky," he recalls, "because I had a teacher who was really passionate about social and environmental issues, so she did a lot of activities with our class, teaching us about the effects that humans have on the environment around us." One of the things she showed them was all the little things they could change in their lives to help fight climate change, like turning off lights and recycling paper.

This alligator was one of Brandon's early influences.
COURTESY OF BRANDON NGUYEN

But Brandon saw that most of the thousands of kids who were going through the Toronto school system hadn't received the same kind of exposure to these ideas. Looking around at his classmates, Brandon saw untapped potential and wanted to do something about it. So in tenth grade he started the Toronto Coalition of EcoSchools (TCE) with a couple of friends to promote **environmental literacy** and awareness across high schools in Toronto.

"Don't be afraid to take risks. And if you do take risks, don't be afraid to seek support. Although you might not think so, friends and family are there to help you and they really do want to help."

Starting TCE was challenging for Brandon. Other students questioned and criticized him. "Lots of people said, 'You're too young. Just focus on school. You don't know what you're doing.'" None of his friends wanted to be environmental activists. He felt alone, but he didn't let that stop him. "Whereas a lot of other people might be discouraged," he says, "it was something I was okay with."

Brandon had been one of the only people in his primary school from an ethnic minority. "I used to bring Asian food for lunch," he remembers, "and I would hate it." The other kids would tease him about it and he felt embarrassed, so he was afraid to take it out of his bag. But he knew they just didn't know any better. As he grew older, he started to ask his parents about what it was like for them growing up in Vietnam and then coming to Canada.

DID YOU KNOW?

The Toronto Coalition of EcoSchools was founded by eight high-school students on a $200 microloan and has since supported more than 30 other environmental clubs.

Brandon organizes a sustainable cooking workshop through the Toronto Coalition of EcoSchools. His goal is to promote the accessibility and affordability of cooking sustainably using things like local produce when possible and finding alternatives to meat.

COURTESY OF BRANDON NGUYEN

Learning more about his cultural heritage made him realize that it wasn't something to be ashamed of, and this made him feel more comfortable with being different from the other students.

"Something my culture has taught me is that differences are okay, and it's okay if you're alone in your beliefs. In the end, if it's something you strongly believe in, that's what matters the most."

So he kept on talking to his friends and family about his passion for the environment. They still didn't see themselves as environmentalists, but they saw how important this work was to Brandon and decided to help. Some of them joined him in leading the organization, and others started to spread the word to people they knew in other parts of the city.

With this support, the TCE expanded to other schools, and Brandon found lots of other young people who were just as passionate about the environment as he was. They hosted workshops and conferences, raised funds for local and national projects, and sent out community ambassadors. By 2017 the TCE had

Brandon (front table, second from left) participates in a municipal advisory meeting run by the Toronto Environmental Alliance. *COURTESY OF BRANDON NGUYEN*

grown to include more than 50 student leaders from more than 30 schools. And in helping him get started, his friends and family had become more interested in environmental issues themselves.

Brandon believes that environmental **sustainability** is important to everyone's life, no matter what their interests are. "You can be a sustainable engineer, a sustainable academic or a sustainable doctor," he explains. "I see sustainability as a lens for observing the world around us."

Working with differences ended up being one of Brandon's major achievements. He organized an annual event called *Sustainable Speaks*, which shows students how everything is connected and that there are things they need to know about the environment no matter which subject they're interested in.

"It goes back to my ultimate goal," Brandon explains. "I want to be able to emphasize that environmental literacy shouldn't be some isolated field of study. Everyone receives a foundational education in math or English. I think everyone should also receive some sort of education in sustainability and environmental literacy."

He started to look for more ways to involve people in his community with environmental issues that affected their daily lives. When he was in 11th grade, he learned that the City of Toronto was looking for members for its youth advisory board, the Toronto Youth Cabinet (TYC). Brandon thought he wasn't qualified, so he almost didn't apply. But he did—and became the TYC's Director of Public Relations. The experience taught him how to use social media to reach out to young people and raise awareness about climate change. It also showed him how important it is for young people to speak up about things they care about.

"Even though we don't have voting powers," he stresses, "we should be voicing our concerns because we're going to have to deal with the consequences of the political decisions that are made today."

"If we give students and future leaders the knowledge and skills to make their own decisions, if they realize how their actions affect the environment around them, that's a great way of fighting climate change."

In 2016 Brandon was a Canadian delegate to the United Nations Youth Assembly in New York City. "There, I was able to represent my organization alongside youth from 80 countries around the world. That gave me a global understanding of climate change." The experience also confirmed for him that youth are an important part of the fight against climate change, especially when they unite.

In 2017 he attended UNLEASH, a global innovation lab held in Denmark that year, which brought together 1,000 people from more than 100 countries and many different organizations to develop solutions to the world's biggest problems. It was a perfect place for him to build a network of other people to work with. Again, though, Brandon was unsure of his abilities. "I thought it was out of my league and I wasn't qualified for it." But he applied and was accepted. At UNLEASH, he learned that the best solutions in one country may not work at all in another. And seeing people from many places sharing their diverse experiences proved to him that a single individual or organization can't accomplish all that is needed to solve global problems; people have to work together.

After finishing high school, Brandon wanted to pull together everything he had learned: how being environmentally responsible is part of everyone's job, how companies and governments work environmental sustainability into their decisions and actions, and how to be an entrepreneur for the environment. He found a business school where he could study economics, environmental policy and management.

Brandon says...

WHAT CAN YOU DO?

"If something is bothering you or if you think something needs to be changed, speak up! Chances are someone else is bothered by it too, but they don't have the courage to speak up. For example, if you learn how bad it is to use plastic water bottles but your family uses them, tell them why using reusable water bottles is better. Little things like that can help."

Brandon in Singapore with his University of Pennsylvania teammates, Avni Limdi, Coco Wang and Angela Yang, at the 2018 Hult Prize Regional Finals, the world's largest social entrepreneurship competition.

COURTESY OF BRANDON NGUYEN

I PRAY
THAT
TOGETHER
WE
ACT
TO PROTECT
OUR SACRED EARTH

Nana Firman in Rome before the 2015 multifaith climate march, called Una terra, una famiglia umana (One Earth, One Human Family), to St. Peter's Square in the Vatican. *NEFA FIRMAN*

Speaking the Language
of Sustainability

NANA FIRMAN

Urban designer and Muslim outreach director
Born in Jambi, Sumatra, Indonesia; lives in Riverside, California

I'm an Indonesian Muslim woman.

Nana Firman says Indonesian cultures are built on nature, which is in abundance there, even in the big city of Jakarta, where she was raised. Local plants like bamboo are used for every-thing—tools, utensils, houses, musical instruments. Food is local and fresh, and clothing is colored with natural dyes. Nana's mom is an avid gardener and has always kept a medicinal plant garden. Her dad designed their house to make sure all the rainwater gets collected and goes back to the earth for future generations.

As a kid, Nana remembers going down a dirt road through the rainforest to visit her grandparents' village on the island of Sumatra. "We saw monkeys jumping in the trees. My mom loves orchids, so I said,

Nana's parents often took her and her siblings to visit their grandparents in Sumatra. Here, Nana and her sister pose at Lembah Anai waterfall, where her family stopped every time.
NOERLEILY RUSLI

'Mom, look at all the orchids on the trees! You can just pick them for free!' I always remember this moment. That was the first time I was exposed to the rainforest."

In the village, they were surrounded by rice fields, mountains and waterfalls. Nana felt as if she were in heaven. She remained fascinated by nature. From Jakarta, she went camping with her Girl Scout troop and joined her high school's nature club. She begged her parents to let her go hiking in the mountains. With the science club, she tried to make perfumes from flowers.

While in high school, Nana spent some time living with a host family in a rural village, helping with their farm and exploring the local mountains. She played and bathed in a river, something she'd never do in the city.

Nana went to university in the United States to study industrial design. In her public speaking class, she gave a speech on Amazonian rainforests. She learned that rainforests are the lungs of the earth, but that in the Amazon they were being destroyed to make cattle ranches to supply meat for McDonald's restaurants. She realized that the same thing could happen in the rainforest country she was from.

"I stopped buying from McDonald's and told other people to stop too. After two years I stopped eating meat. I was not an environmentalist. I didn't know that later in my life I was going to work in environmental groups."

After a massive earthquake and tsunami hit Indonesia in 2004, Nana went back there to help with humanitarian efforts. While she was on a break, she phoned a girlfriend to go for lunch, but somehow she dialed a different friend instead—a man who was the executive director of World Wildlife Fund (WWF) Indonesia.

"Maybe it was by chance. Maybe it was meant to be. He said, 'Come to a meeting tomorrow.' So I went into the office and they said, 'This is your team.' I said, 'What team?' They tricked me! It was a wonderful trick that I'm thankful for every day."

Nana's friend knew she was working in urban design and planning, skills that their environmental team didn't have. He asked her to take her team to the province of Aceh, where the tsunami had hit hard, carrying the ocean far inland. Communities in Aceh—including local WWF staff—were totally overwhelmed by injury and loss of life, as well as damage to buildings. Since WWF is an environmental organization, the staff didn't know much about rebuilding after a disaster.

Nana thought she would be working on the project for four months, but she stayed for four years to lead a program with multiple humanitarian agencies for sustainable reconstruction.

Nana and her team plant mangroves to protect the coastline in Nias Island, Sumatra, as part of the Green Coast Project and Green Reconstruction Program after the earthquakes and tsunamis in 2004 and 2005. *MUHAMMAD ILMAN*

Nana and her husband plant seedlings in the Aceh rainforest. Local people have initiated a conservation program, using an Islamic legal tool called a waqf, to protect that forest from degradation. *AKMAL SENJA*

"The tendency after a disaster," Nana explains, "is to go fast, just rebuild, put everybody back in a house, not paying attention to where the resources come from."

About 500,000 people lost their homes in the tsunami, and reconstruction agencies needed 800,000 cubic meters of timber. That's 320 Olympic-sized swimming pools full of wood! Relief agencies wanted to get the wood from Aceh's pristine rainforests. Nana and her team said no. If the forests on the hillsides were cut down, the soil would erode and smother the towns below. If coastal forests were cut down, there would be even less natural protection if another tsunami happened. They wanted to make sure the wood was from sustainable sources.

"That was my first test," Nana says. "The agencies thought we were stopping reconstruction, but we weren't. We were trying to show people other options. People said it's impossible, these are ridiculous ideas. We said we'll show them it's doable."

They asked sustainable timber associations around the world to donate timber instead of money. They asked shipping companies to ship for free, and other companies to pay for shipping. They managed to bring several shipping containers full of sustainably sourced timber that they gave to organizations for rebuilding.

"They built such beautiful houses," Nana recalls. "Even I wanted to have one."

Seeing this success, other organizations started to use sustainable timber too, even for some of the biggest projects. The houses are still standing, and some have become community centers.

"If I feel down in any of my work, if the challenge is too great, I always go back to that moment," Nana says. "So many were against us, but we worked and in the end everyone understood and everything happened smoothly. They still have the intact forest in Aceh. It's my inspiration, and it has kept me doing what I'm doing until now."

One of the major challenges Nana faced while doing that work was trying to engage with the community. She first started talking to them using jargon from the environmental world, words like *sustainability* and *conservation*. People didn't get what she was talking about, and she got frustrated.

A friend pointed out to her that the Acehnese are a strong Muslim community and suggested that she talk about the issues

DID YOU KNOW?
There's a tradition in Aceh that when a baby is born, the father plants a hardwood tree. By the time the person is old enough to move into their own house, they can use that tree to build it.

from an Islamic perspective. Nana found that the Qur'an says those who serve God walk upon the earth gently, meaning they don't pollute, take more than they need or leave a big *ecological* footprint. It also says that the Creator made people as stewards upon the earth, meaning we have to make sure the earth is unharmed.

When she spoke about environmental issues from the point of view of Islamic teachings, people felt a connection with their traditions and beliefs and wanted to be part of the project. That sparked a passion in Nana, and she started to explore it more. She found a mentor—Fazlun Khalid, who is the founder of the Islamic Foundation for Ecology and Environmental Sciences in the United Kingdom.

Nana realized that this was what she was being called for. "Protecting and caring for the earth is part of my worship to my Creator."

Returning to the United States, and fasting during the sacred month of Ramadan, she noticed that her local mosques broke the fast using disposable plates and utensils. She discussed this with the Imam, saying that, as Muslims, they were not supposed to be producing all that waste. He asked her to speak to the community directly. She talked about environmental protection and climate

---

Nana says...

WHAT CAN YOU DO?

"Be part of a green club. Learn how to plant food, simple vegetables that you eat every day. Plant something, then take care of it. Take a walk in nature and reflect. Ask your parents to take you camping."

change from an Islamic perspective. The community immediately understood and started to make changes. Nana had initiated Green Ramadan with a local Muslim community in San Diego.

"The Imam then told other mosques to invite me to talk to their communities," she recalls. "A few years later, the board of the Islamic Center of San Diego agreed to install solar panels in our mosque. Meanwhile, the Islamic Society of North America formed a green mosque task force."

The Muslim women's magazine *Azizah* asked Nana to write an article about climate change and featured her on the cover of the issue. Then an organization called GreenFaith, which trains environmental leaders

"I didn't force it and say, 'You have to change,' but I asked, 'What can you do within your community? Please do something, even a small step.'"

Participants in the 2017 People's Climate March in Washington, DC, sat on the streets around the White House to recognize people who had lost their lives to climate change. They tapped a heartbeat rhythm on their chests to show that their hearts beat as one. *COURTESY OF NANA FIRMAN*

from different faiths, asked her to join their fellowship program—and later asked her to be their Muslim outreach director.

She then helped form the Global Muslim Climate Network, with the major goals of transforming mosques so they can use **renewable energy** and educating Muslim communities about climate change **mitigation**. She's brought together Islamic scholars, energy experts and financial specialists to develop solutions together.

"Young people have the right to inherit good conditions. They need to say what sort of future they hope for and demand that adults take responsibility."

Nana has been able to connect with people from many different places through her own connection with nature. "When I talk about nature, I always relate to where I'm from," she says. "It's in my blood and my bones. People who come from nature feel a connection—like telepathy. I might not speak their language, but we recognize something in each other."

She wants to reach out more, to convince decision-makers that we need to change unsustainable lifestyles to protect the earth and future generations. In the meantime, some decision-makers have taken notice of her work.

In 2015 Nana got a phone call from the White House. At first she thought it was a prank caller and said, "Yeah, right." They told her she had been nominated for President Obama's Champion of Change program, which recognized people who were making

DID YOU KNOW?
Green Ramadan is now recognized by the Islamic Society of North America and by Muslim communities around the globe.

a difference in their communities. When she got the award, the news went viral, especially in Indonesia. It was such a whirlwind that Nana hardly understood what had happened. But it confirmed that she was doing the right thing with her life.

"The path is there, grabbing me and pulling me," she says. "I feel blessed that I get to do what I love and am passionate about, and that I found my voice."

Muslims led the Keepers of Faith multifaith contingent at the 2017 People's Climate March in Washington, DC. Muslim-majority countries are some of the most severely affected by climate change. *AUBREY GEMIGNANI*

Getting Your Outdoor Afro On

RUE MAPP

Founder and chief executive officer, Outdoor Afro
Born and lives in Oakland, California

I identify as an African American woman and mother.

Rue Mapp's family spent every other weekend on their ranch north of Oakland, California, where Rue grew up. There, Rue rode her bike everywhere, played by a local creek and watched what changed around her with the seasons. She grew vegetables, took care of animals, hunted and fished. She remembers the smells of fresh air and of leaves as they fell and turned to compost, and the contrast between snowy winters and hot summers at a nearby lake. With free time in nature, experiencing wonder, discovery and awe, Rue learned to love the outdoors. She also loved spending her outdoor time with others.

Rue spent a lot of time outdoors with her family when she was growing up.
RUE MAPP/OUTDOOR AFRO

"It wasn't about going out and being in nature by myself," she remembers, "but being in a community of all ages and seeing the importance of that community using nature as a place of retreat and a place of connection."

As she got older, Rue looked for more nature-based experiences. From camping as a Girl Scout to mountaineering as part of a wilderness education program, she let nature be her teacher and show her how strong she really was. She remembers, during her first time rock climbing, being stuck on the side of a mountain, unable to see her way up or down and beginning to panic. She heard her instructor's voice above her: "Trust your feet." Those three words propelled her up the mountain and forward in her life.

"The outdoors is a part of everyone's lives. Even if you go to your neighborhood park, or you have a balcony, nature is everywhere. You don't have to hang off the side of a cliff to have your nature activities. You can be gardening or learning how to identify birds."

"From that moment on," she says, "I knew I had everything I needed inside of me to succeed in nature."

Rue went on to have children of her own, and she continued her family tradition by sharing the outdoors with them.

Throughout her life, Rue had noticed that African Americans weren't represented in popular images of outdoor activities, among neither the leaders nor the participants. On their adventures, she and her family rarely came across other people who looked like them or who reflected the diversity of people who live in the United States.

African Americans' history with the outdoors is complex and unique. Many are the descendants of people who had been enslaved. During the slavery era, many were forced to work on plantations and were brutalized while contributing to the building of America with their bare hands. After slavery was abolished,

African Americans were still under constant threat of being beaten, jailed, raped, lynched, mobbed or murdered, often in rural and wooded areas. Once African Americans had some freedom to enjoy leisure activities, the US government developed segregation policies, called Jim Crow laws, that excluded them from many outdoor recreational places. As a result, for many African Americans, wilderness areas have been places not of peace but of terror.

Within this history, through living in rural areas, many African Americans developed an understanding of weather, seasons, plant medicines, and food growing, along with many other qualities and skills. As the years and decades advanced, however, a lot of people migrated from rural to urban areas. All that and more shaped how African Americans connect with nature today.

Rue dreamed of seeing people who looked like her benefiting from nature in the same ways that she had. African Americans paid taxes, and she wanted them to feel that they owned public lands, particularly wild lands, as much as any other American.

After years of working in finance, Rue thought about going back to school, but she wasn't sure what she should do. One day, a friend asked her what she would do with her life if time and money weren't a barrier, if she could do anything she wanted.

DID YOU KNOW?

Even when US policies excluded them from going to many recreation sites, African Americans still found ways to have fun outside. This included Black beaches, Black ski resorts and Black areas in tourism destinations such as Martha's Vineyard.

"I opened my mouth and my life fell out," Rue says matter-of-factly. "I said, 'Oh, I'd probably start a website to reconnect African Americans with the outdoors.' It was a surprise for my friend, but it was a moment of truth for me."

After that conversation, Rue started a blog from her kitchen table, calling it *Outdoor Afro*. At first she wrote short posts almost every day, with simple suggestions to help people start biking, camping and exploring local forests with their families. Then she started telling her own story, talking about obstacles African Americans might be experiencing, and introducing topics that could spark discussion. This all happened when social media was relatively new. Rue learned about and tried different techniques to reach more people. The lists of comments in response to her blog posts got longer.

"I found that many people who looked like me wanted to connect with the outdoors," Rue says. "*Outdoor Afro* became a resource for people to find other people to get outside with."

All the aspects of Rue's background—her race, her connection with the outdoors, her comfort using technology—combined to give her the tools to relate to, interact with and inspire a segment of the population that other environmentalists had ignored.

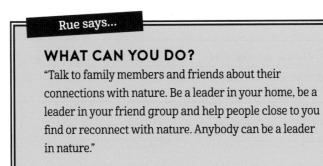

Rue says...

WHAT CAN YOU DO?

"Talk to family members and friends about their connections with nature. Be a leader in your home, be a leader in your friend group and help people close to you find or reconnect with nature. Anybody can be a leader in nature."

Organizing a group outdoor activity like hiking or snowboarding, and helping people prepare for it, is one way to get people into nature. *OUTDOOR AFRO*

Rue added posts from other "Outdoor Afros" who had stories, opportunities or advice to share. She started organizing public events and participating in national activities, including the president's conference on conservation. She transformed her blog and the activities that arose from it into a nonprofit organization, and she was able to apply for national grants and sponsorships that allowed her to run the organization as her paid job.

As a community, Rue and her fellow Outdoor Afros learned about additional reasons why more African Americans weren't going outdoors. Some people didn't know what gear they would need, some were worried about what people they met in the outdoors might do or say to them, some were afraid of critters that could bite them or crawl on them, and some didn't have a means of transportation or the time to get anywhere wild.

Traditional environmental and conservation movements have focused on places and not people, says Rue. Outdoor Afro is about people and places, people and nature, and people with nature. *OUTDOOR AFRO*

The people involved with Outdoor Afro understood all the social, political, psychological and practical barriers that African Americans face—and how deeply rooted they are. "That's when we decided to create our leadership team and lower those barriers for people," Rue says.

Within a few years, Outdoor Afro had grown well beyond Rue, her computer and her kitchen table. It became a **collective** with a dozen leaders in different parts of the country who organized events for African Americans to enjoy the outdoors together. They saw that to address complex issues, they had to develop complex strategies. They moved beyond getting more African Americans outside to training people to become what Rue calls "change-makers."

"By change-makers," she explains, "I mean people who learn about not only leading in the outdoors but what it means to hold a space of hospitality and *social justice* in this work." These individuals weave together the practical support needed to enable African Americans to get outdoors, lead conversations about nature conservation, build community and help people feel that wild spaces are not places of terror and exclusion but places where they can find comfort and healing.

"We create leadership in a space that feels safe and welcoming, while having a regard for protecting vulnerable places. That's what makes us different."

Outdoor Afro gives people access to nature to help them gain strength. It has organized Healing Hikes across the country to help people deal with despair and distrust following repeated incidents of police brutality. Yoga, art, walks, discussions and commitments made in nature have been the organization's method of nonviolent protest and a road forward.

Outdoor Afro now has 70 leaders in 28 states who are making careers of being in the outdoors, guiding thousands of people through nature-based experiences and helping them have environmentally friendly lifestyles. This amazes even Rue. "It's phenomenal to see how we've grown from storytelling into a respected national network that is really helping to change the face of outdoor leadership."

DID YOU KNOW?

You don't need an afro to join. Although Outdoor Afro is focused on the African American experience, it has a connection with everyone. Nature doesn't discriminate, and neither does Outdoor Afro.

Rue has won many awards and honors from the outdoor industry, wildlife conservation societies, *Family Circle* magazine and African American organizations. This diverse list demonstrates how many important issues she has combined in her work. How satisfying is that?

> "Follow your dreams. Even if you don't see what you want to be represented in the world, you can create it."

"The thing about this work that's so important for me is that it allows me as a Black woman who's a mom living in America to be fully expressed in leadership and gives me a chance to help improve people's lives through connections to nature," Rue says. "What makes it so successful is how personally fulfilling it is."

Nature is a powerful teacher and a place in which to build strength. Rue says that we can all find our own way in nature. *OUTDOOR AFRO*

Outdoor Afro enables and empowers African American people to get into wild spaces. *OUTDOOR AFRO*

A rare shot of Ismail Ebrahim in the office—he'd rather be outside. *GIGI LAIDLER*

Treasure Hunting

ISMAIL EBRAHIM

Project manager
Born and lives in Cape Town, South Africa

I'm a South African Muslim.

As far as Ismail Ebrahim knew, his life had been planned for him from birth. He watched his older siblings carry on the family tradition set out by their father, a successful businessman in Cape Town. When each sibling came of age, they were given a business to manage. Maybe his father saw something else in Ismail, or maybe he just thought Ismail wouldn't be so great at business, but when Ismail graduated from high school, his father encouraged him to continue his education.

"I'd never thought about what I'd do after school or what I'd study because I thought it wasn't an option," Ismail recalls. He went to a career center with his buddies and looked through a book about different degrees and diplomas. The things he was most interested in required him to have taken physics in school, which he hadn't.

Ismail gets ready for a future as a specialist in rare and endangered plants.
COURTESY OF ISMAIL EBRAHIM

"After going through 30 pages, I said, 'The next thing I see where you don't need physics, I'm doing that.' Three pages on, there was a horticulture diploma, so I filled in the form and sent it. I started the program without the slightest clue what it was all about. I think it was fate that took me to horticulture and eventually got me to where I am today."

As part of his program, Ismail worked at an agricultural research center studying a group of rare and showy flowers called proteas, which are part of a unique group of plants called fynbos. Then he did an internship to help map areas where proteas were growing. He worked with volunteers who spent their spare time going into remote areas all over southern Africa to record where they saw rare species. Sometimes they found plants that only a few people had ever seen, which really got Ismail excited.

"Now I think of myself as an ambassador for conservation, but when I was growing up I couldn't care less," Ismail says. "The closest interaction I had with nature growing up was looking after my dog. I basically spent life working Sunday to Sunday in a shop. After being in a very sheltered, routine environment where I never went out to do anything, that initial exposure to being out in the wild and experiencing this flora [plant life] was amazing for me. It was completely new. Being with people who were passionate about the environment changed my ideas."

After his internship was over, Ismail went back to work in his family's businesses, which confirmed for him that running

Moraea atropunctata is one of Ismail's favorite plants. It's known to exist only in a few sites on a single farm. Its population is in decline due to overgrazing and flower picking. *ISMAIL EBRAHIM*

a shop was not what he wanted to do with his life. He missed doing fieldwork—being out in nature, looking at plants. He started looking for work and was hired by a conservation organization to coordinate a project called Custodians of Rare and Endangered Wildflowers (CREW). For Ismail, it was the best job in the world.

"There's a massive amount of fieldwork. You work with amazing volunteers and amazing flora. It's something I'm really passionate about. That's why, 15 years on, it's like day one in the project. And the job's not done yet. We still have tonnes of species

DID YOU KNOW?

The fynbos ecosystem is found only in the Cape region of South Africa. It includes several plants that only grow in very specific areas.

Ismail's colleagues work in the field to identify plants and search for rare and endangered species.
ISMAIL EBRAHIM

to monitor and many under-explored areas to visit."

Leading CREW, Ismail set up 12 volunteer groups to search for threatened plants so they could be protected. "It's a bit like treasure hunting. We give them the descriptions and pictures of the threatened plants. Then they go out and look," Ismail explains. "Finding rare species has become a bit of an addiction for me."

Because the volunteers are out looking, they've found new species. They've also rediscovered species that people thought had gone extinct, including one that was last seen in the 1800s. They help keep the national and international lists of threatened and endangered plants up to date and can say which areas have a lot of sites that are important to conserve.

Their work has revealed the most endangered group of plants in South Africa, called *Marasmodes*, an otherwise inconspicuous group of shrubs. They started what Ismail calls a botanical holiday, coinciding with South Africa's national Freedom Day. For Ismail and his plant-loving volunteers, it's *Marasmodes* Day. On that day, volunteers look for new locations of these plants and search for species that haven't been seen for a long time.

"We've done fantastically well in raising the profile of some inconspicuous things that are highly threatened and in need of conservation but that don't normally grab the public's attention," Ismail says.

Many rare plants are found on private property, so Ismail and the volunteers also work with landowners to inspire them to take care of the areas where those plants grow. But going onto private property to look for plants hasn't been easy for Ismail.

He entered the world of conservation soon after the end of apartheid in South Africa. Apartheid was the policy that segregated people by race in favor of the white minority, discriminating against the non-white majority. For a person of color, leading mostly white volunteers and entering white landowners' properties was difficult. Early in his career, Ismail felt a lot of pressure to prove that he deserved his job, because apartheid made people believe that non-white people were less intelligent. Also, many people were still openly racist in the rural areas where he worked. Some of the landowners carried weapons as they approached him.

"The more environmentally savvy you are, and the more you interact with nature, the more you'll be able to forge an environmentally sound future."

I asked Ismail what kept him going despite these challenges.

"The love for the work," he replied. "I felt it was something worth taking a few racist comments and gestures for. Also, Islam teaches that you should have patience and perseverance when you are faced with challenges, because you come out stronger and with blessings from God."

DID YOU KNOW?

Fynbos plants need fire to recycle nutrients back into the soil so they can grow. Some species appear only in the first year or two after a fire, then disappear until the next fire.

Since those early beginnings, Ismail has worked with a steady stream of volunteers. Keeping them involved and inspired has required acceptance of differing views, which he also learned from his Muslim faith. He's built a strong and extensive network, one relationship at a time, sometimes having to be the person in the middle when volunteers don't see eye to eye. "For me, it's about conservation and protecting the environment, so I try to maintain peace with everyone."

In learning more about conservation and his religion, Ismail found that Islam teaches that humans have a responsibility to look after the earth and its resources, be kind to animals and plants, and not be wasteful or cut down trees or other plants unnecessarily. That's brought his work to an even deeper level.

"You feel that you can connect and relate to what you believe in when you're out there in nature, seeing the creation of God, interacting with it and contributing to protecting it," he says. "It has a deep religious and spiritual meaning, the work that we do."

Ismail wants more people to get outdoors and really experience nature as he has, to increase their understanding and appreciation for it. It's only when we see how we're part of the ecosystems around us, he says, that we realize how our actions affect them. "We need to spread the message. The more people are

DID YOU KNOW?

The diversity of species within a fynbos area can be three times more than the diversity in a tropical rainforest.

Ismail shares his passion for rare plants and the area's unique fynbos ecosystems with students from the Cape Peninsula University of Technology. *GIGI LAIDLER*

out there looking for these threatened plants and protecting the areas where they occur, the better chance we have of conserving and protecting these species."

Ismail says...

WHAT CAN YOU DO?

"Go out and experience nature. The more observant you are, the more exciting the ride becomes. Look at a plant as something more than leaves and flowers and you will be fascinated. Question and experience and experiment. Enjoy this time of life, when you can be carefree and outside, exploring in nature."

Two

DEFENDING LANDS AND WATERS

Our forest is our temple, says Flávio Santi Ayuy Yú. APRIL LIU

Protecting Ancient Relationships

FLÁVIO SANTI AYUY YÚ

Healer

Born and lives in La Comuna Campesina de San Jacinto de Davila, Ecuador, in the territory of the Puyukruna (People of the Spirit of the High Mountain Clouds)

We are Ayuy Yú—the Spirit of the Palm. We are medicine people of the forest, of our land. Our identity claims a low profile: the gardening child, the sweeping child and the firewood child. This is the path to becoming a yachak—learned one, shaman, healer.

"Sometimes we don't have maturity even at 20 or 25 years old, but I had it as a teenager." Flávio Santi Ayuy Yú isn't bragging. He's telling the reality of his youth, life and continued struggle.

Flávio's ancestors took care of two million hectares of rainforest for many generations. They lacked nothing and enjoyed clean air and water, and plenty of food. Around them were the sounds of birds and waterfalls. Protecting their relationship with the land so it would give them what they would need for centuries to come was what they considered to be "development."

In 1915 the oil industry began to arrive in their area, with the support of the military. Flávio's grandfather, a medicine man, fought against this **colonization** during a 30-year war and was shot. The military targeted medicine people and activists.

"They founded cities on top of our communities," Flávio explains, "and contaminated our land, our rivers. The development of destruction had arrived."

When Flávio was 15 years old, his family moved from their hunting territory deep in the jungle to their comuna (community in their territory), which was closer to a big town. They had heard that the government was trying to stop Indigenous communities from managing their land collectively, so they emerged to defend their rights.

Flávio found himself faced with choices that he summarizes as one circle with two halves, light and dark. The dark half included some very bad things—crime, violence, drugs and alcohol—but also offered work and the promise of money. To make people believe that they had community support,

Flávio and his three children raise their arms and open a portal at the waterfall near the site where they are creating the Wayusa School. Wayusa is an Amazon rainforest plant used for promoting good health, understanding dreams and uplifting emotions. It is called cushipanga (leaf of joy) in the Indigenous Kichwa language.
ANDREA DAVIS

oil companies tried to hire Indigenous people, including Flávio. The other half—the light half—came through dreams of his already deceased grandfather, who told Flávio to be true to what he was: a gardening child, a guardian of the territory and the culture. But Flávio knew it would be a lifelong commitment—and a dangerous one, as his grandfather's experience had shown him.

One day, he was with a family whose teenage daughter was dying. There were no other shamans nearby. Flávio decided to do a spiritual cleansing and bring out the negative spirits that were making her sick. It was the first time he had ever tried anything like it. And it worked.

Word got out and many called him to heal people and perform other spiritual work. But Flávio was afraid of his abilities and afraid of failing. He went to another town and started selling crafts, trying to escape his fear and the responsibility of being a healer. But his father and uncle found him and told him that his community needed him. They brought him home and began to train him to be a young leader.

At 16, Flávio became the community's spokesperson, a link between the Elder shamans and the government. He began doing what his heart told him he had to do: heal people and protect the land, water and air.

When Flávio was 19, he and the other medicine people foresaw something terrible. "We dreamed that monsters were

> "My recommendation to the leaders and the children of the world is to ask and decide: What are your roots? Where do you come from? What is your purpose? What is the human footprint that you're leaving on this land? This is the principle for decision-making."

"The spirit of the blue macaw is the spirit of the mother and the father, protecting their children who are part of the struggle," says Flávio. "So I was playing this song with the flute, and now we weren't only 2,000 Indigenous people marching, we were more than 25,000." *COURTESY OF MONKEYTOWN FILMS, IMAGE BY PIETER STATHIS, CSC*

going to arrive through the clouds, through the wind," he recalls. "The stars, the ancestors, they advised us to protect our water. And the monsters arrived."

Three years later, in the early 1990s, oil companies began to expand their operations in his community's territory. The military, which was supporting the companies, destroyed Indigenous people's homes, and the government publicly distorted their image by saying their cultivation of medicinal plants meant they were growing illegal drugs. Meanwhile, oil exploration and extraction were causing severe air, ground and water pollution and making people sick.

"They called us lazy Indians. They said we didn't want to work the land and we didn't want development." Flávio says that's not true. "We have a distinct version of development that includes the waterfalls and the trees. We're rich. We have knowledge, culture, language, medicines, fish for our children. That's what they were destroying—our wealth."

At a large meeting, Flávio and other leaders called for war, but the women convinced them that a peaceful demonstration would be better, as too many had died already. Flávio helped the indigenous-led Organización de los Pueblos Indígenas del Pastaza organize a march for life and land to the capital city. In his toucan headdress and feathers, with traditional tattoos across his face, he was among 2,000 Indigenous people who started marching from the Amazon jungle in 1992, 155 miles up and over the Andean mountains to Quito.

"We walked for a month to shout to the nation and the world that we want title to our lands and that, with or without title, we are the owners of these lands."

Many of the people marching had never before left their homelands in the warmth of the Amazon, so the steep climb and the change in elevation and temperature were overwhelming. The skin on their faces broke open from the cold mountain air. Their shoes wore out on the pavement. Many people became sick along the way,

---

Flávio says...

WHAT CAN YOU DO?

"Sing. Learn to sing songs of the water, the stars, the mountains. Sing for the rising of the sun. Sing for the setting of the sun. This has many meanings: the connection with our ancestors, mothers and fathers, brothers, sisters, partners. Everything we do today with our technology, the grandparents did with flutes and the rays of the sun. There's magic in songs."

Being humble is how Flávio's people maintain balance as guardians in their relationship with the land, universe, sacred places, lagoons and waterfalls. *KESTER REID*

and Flávio and others had to heal them using traditional medicine.

Flávio stops talking for a moment to play a melody on his flute, the melody he had played while marching. To me, it sounds like birds singing to each other across the forest canopy.

Different Indigenous nations joined at every city, and the march grew to more than 25,000 people. In response, the government granted some land rights to some Indigenous communities—but not the group rights they had been asking for or the rights to anything underground, where the oil reserves lie. The government used this strategy and others to fragment this growing movement.

Yet Indigenous people continued to speak out, even though they put their lives at risk doing so. "Fighting in my territory is difficult," Flávio explains. "They begin to persecute you if there are no friends from outside who can criticize what they're doing." Although they didn't get everything they were demanding, Indigenous people in Ecuador were finally beginning to be heard, including by international media.

Flávio was invited to speak at a conference in the United States. It was his first opportunity to tell an international audience about his people's struggle. Not only were they willing to listen, but they wanted to help. The Indigenous movement started to gain a lot of support from other countries. Sadly, it didn't last.

In 1997 and 1998, Flávio's community took the oil companies to court over a planned pipeline that would go through their land.

The community lost the court battle and the judge exposed the fact that many Indigenous leaders had become corrupt—the companies had bought their support. Learning this, many international allies stopped helping. The pipeline was built.

"I went to see the territory of my grandfather. It was destroyed, the river contaminated. My house had been destroyed." Flávio begins to cry as he recounts this story, and I cry too. "There had been many parrots, it was beautiful—a paradise. I grew up there running with my grandfather, drinking **wayusa** (a medicinal tea) from the mountain."

Flávio saw that environmental destruction meant the genocide of Indigenous Peoples. He became depressed and enraged. He wanted to start an armed uprising. But Elders took him aside and told him that the spirit of conflict was making him sick. He was becoming like those he was fighting. "Let them destroy the territory," they told him. "Don't let them destroy you."

> *"We're a lot of consumers in a world that just accepts everything. We should return to a world that decides to put plants in the ground and visit rivers, lagoons, waterfalls. For each day we walk into the light, breathe the air, step on the earth, the land deserves our offering."*

His Elders cleansed him and he went back to the spiritual teachings, plant medicines and visions, and his connection with his ancestors. He decided to fight with the spirit, not weapons. In doing so, he again had to make a difficult choice.

One of the things Flávio's family had taught him was that the world around him is a temple that doesn't belong to any company or person.

"Since my youth, I've fought to not break their word, to not sell land, water or trees," he says, before telling me about his people's recent achievement. The only way they could protect any part of their territory was to buy it—even though they had never sold it or given it away. "It gives us great sadness to buy our own land."

After 24 years of struggle, Flávio and his family, with the help of international allies, recovered 5,000 acres, which is 80 percent of the sacred sites his grandfather had foreseen they would need to take back. Part of that land is now protected as a reserve called the Eternal Forest of the Children. They are also setting up the Wayusa School to teach ancient wisdom in a modern way to local children and international visitors. They continue their fight to protect their lands, waters and knowledge from being bought and sold by people who don't respect their importance to future generations.

"They call us poor. They label us so they can manipulate us. It should be announced to the world that those who live at the edges of this dominant culture, whether they're Indigenous people or Black people, are rich. We have our connection with our culture, with Pacha Mama (Universal Mother) and Jawa Pacha (Sky Universe). Poor are those who destroy the butterflies, the waterfalls, our sacred sites—those who don't recognize true wealth."

DID YOU KNOW?

The ancestors of today's Indigenous Shuar people played a game where they would dive into a lake and bring a sleeping caiman (an animal like an alligator) to the surface without waking it or making it react, then take it back down. This showed that warriors are strong if they have such a positive attitude toward other beings that they can earn the respect of even the most aggressive animal. The warriors don't win a prize; they win the trust of the animal, the land and the spirits.

Flávio and his family work to recover and protect his people's ancestral lands and sacred sites that were taken from them for oil development and the wave of settlement that followed.
KESTER REID

Ken Wu loves nature and ecosystems—groups of interconnected animals, plants and other organisms, and their environments. To him, the most spectacular ecosystems are old-growth forests. *CURTIS ANDREWS*

Saving Giants

KEN WU

Executive director, Ancient Forest Alliance
Born in Ottawa, Ontario; lives in Victoria, British Columbia

I identify myself as Canadian or Taiwanese Canadian.

Ken Wu's dad used to take him fishing in southern Ontario and Saskatchewan. While his dad set out his line, Ken combed the shoreline, searching for frogs and watching them jump into the lake as he approached. When they were in Saskatchewan, he searched through prairie grasslands to find badgers chasing ground squirrels. When he was four, Ken began to go to a local pond in the suburbs of Toronto to look at the toads and frogs that lived there. Two years later, developers bulldozed that pond and the area around it.

Ken with his sister in Toronto, ON. Ken's skinned knees are evidence of his early habitat explorations.
COURTESY OF KEN WU

"I thought about all the frogs suffocating to death under the soil and mud," he remembers. "That changed me. I became determined to protect nature."

He began staying late in his school library, reading books about nature.

The more he read about *ecology* and the environment, the more passionate he became.

One day, his dad gave him a book about the Pacific coast of Canada. In it, there was a picture of people dancing on a giant stump while men in handlebar mustaches played the violin. "It made my imagination go wild," he says. He wondered if any trees that big were still alive; then he found out that they were.

Ken saw his first *old-growth forest* on a family trip to British Columbia. Seeing the spectacular trees and the moss and plants hanging off them like something out of a movie set ignited his passion to save these forests. In high school he became involved in campaigns to save British Columbia's iconic old-growth forests in the Carmanah Valley, Haida Gwaii and the Walbran Valley, and eventually he moved to the West Coast of Canada to study ecology.

Ken's parents had immigrated to Canada from Taiwan, which had been occupied by a foreign military force from the 1940s until the 1990s. This history has led many Taiwanese people to be

When an old-growth tree is left to die naturally and fall over, it provides homes for a multitude of creatures and nurtures new plants. In this photo, Ken is showing us the root wad of a fallen giant. *CURTIS ANDREWS*

politically minded. His parents talked about politics and activism all the time while he was growing up.

"That made it natural," he explains, "that later on I would become political for what I really cared most about, which was nature."

Raised in Taiwanese culture, which places a heavy emphasis on studying and working hard, Ken developed the habit of reading and learning a lot about anything he wanted to work on. Although studying didn't seem like much fun when he was younger, he thinks that habit ended up making him a better environmentalist.

"Being wrong and being passionate as an activist is horrible," he says. "The more you learn and read, the better."

> "Try to see things from others' perspectives. Keep learning from others. The more you learn from others, the stronger you can legitimately become in the positions you ultimately arrive at."

As a Taiwanese Canadian, Ken feels quite different from many of the people involved in the current environmental activist culture in Canada. Because of that, it's easy for him to see things from other perspectives and connect with different kinds of people. He believes that having people in the environmental movement with different backgrounds increases its power to make change.

"The environmental movement has typically been engaging its own kind," he laments. Ken realized early on that talking only to other people who are like you won't change things on a large scale, especially when it comes to changing economic priorities that end up being bad for the environment. So Ken does his work differently. As part of the Ancient Forest Alliance, which Ken co-founded with his friend TJ Watt, he works with businesses, chambers of commerce, pulp and paper unions, forestry workers, multicultural groups, faith groups and outdoor recreation groups to broaden

Ken has made it his life's work to cooperate with others to find and save ancient forests such as this one. *CURTIS ANDREW*

his organization's reach. Because governments pay more attention to messages from a wide range of voters, the Ancient Forest Alliance's **inclusivity** has brought about real change both on the ground and in the woods.

In 2010 Ken and TJ were looking for stands of old-growth forest, which is something they do regularly as part of their work. Near the fishing and logging town of Port Renfrew, on Vancouver Island, they went to an area that was marked with flagging tape and scheduled to be clear-cut. They looked around at the massive western red cedar and Douglas fir trees in one of the few unlogged old-growth forests in a low-lying area. Ken saw an opportunity to bring people to see these majestic trees firsthand, help to save the trees and contribute to the local economy—all at the same time. He noticed that Port Renfrew was ripe for transition; it had accommodations, restaurants and other businesses that would flourish if more tourists came to the area. So he had two things to figure out:

how to get tourists to go there and how to keep that forest from being cut down.

When he went home that night, Ken decided they needed to create a catchy name for that stand of giant trees to make people interested in it. "This movie had just come out," he remembers, "about saving a forest, albeit on an alien moon." That movie was *Avatar*. So he started calling the area Avatar Grove. Now he needed a campaign to save it. He knew they wouldn't be able to save this old-growth stand and then others if it was only environmental groups who launched the campaign. So Ken and TJ reached out to the local business community. After many meetings and conversations, the businesses of Port Renfrew joined the call to protect Avatar Grove.

The Ancient Forest Alliance and the Port Renfrew business community began to work together on projects that would help both their causes, like holding a fund-raiser with the local Chamber of Commerce to raise money to hire someone to work at a tourism kiosk. The booth included information about the local motorcycle route, ocean areas and walks through the ancient forest. Because it showed that people could do many different things in Port Renfrew, it encouraged tourists to come back again and again.

> **Ken says...**
>
> ## WHAT CAN YOU DO?
> "Make sure your parents and school only buy paper that's been certified by the Forest Stewardship Council and wood products that are sourced from more sustainably managed forests. Organize a nature club where students can learn about animals and plants, write letters to the government asking to protect them, learn about conservation and do nature walks."

For two years the Ancient Forest Alliance and Port Renfrew put pressure on the government, calling for Avatar Grove to be protected. They hit the headlines more than a hundred times in provincial, national and even international news outlets. "This raised the profile to a breaking point," says Ken. What made a huge difference was the support of the business community, which the government paid a lot of attention to. Finally, in 2012, the government of British Columbia announced the protection of Avatar Grove.

"Learn about the environment well. Get other people to learn about it, then get everyone to speak their minds to the political decision-makers. Or get involved in politics and become the political decision-makers."

When Ken first started working to save old-growth forests as a teenager, only 2 percent of them were protected. Almost 30 years later that number increased to about 10 percent. By collaborating with others, Ken Wu has been involved in campaigns leading to the protection of almost 20 million acres of old-growth forest.

DID YOU KNOW?

The tallest tree recorded in British Columbia's Big Tree Registry in 2018 was a 315-foot Sitka spruce known as the Carmanah Giant because it is in the Carmanah Valley west of the town of Lake Cowichan. The tree is about the height of eight *Tyrannosaurus rex* dinosaurs.

Ken and TJ named a western red cedar in Avatar Grove "Canada's Gnarliest Tree" because of its huge and contorted burl (a wooden lump formed if a tree gets infected by a fungus or virus or if it needs to store cells to help regenerate after being damaged by windstorms). *CURTIS ANDREWS*

Willi Nolan-Campbell at a Wabanaki Confederacy Indigenous gathering in 2015. *MELODY WALKER BROOK*

Uniting for Clean Water

WILLI NOLAN-CAMPBELL

Activist and ecopreneur
Born in K'jipuktuk (Halifax, Nova Scotia);
resides in Sikinuiktuk (Kent County, New Brunswick) and
Accompong Maroon Sovereign State (Jamaica)

*I am a human woman, identified by the communities
I serve as a Grandmother and an Elder.*

"I have always loved being in nature," Willi Nolan-Campbell says. "I remember promising myself that one day I'd live next to the trees and the bears. And I did."

Even in the big city of Toronto, Ontario, where Willi was raised, her mother had always made sure that she and her siblings had fun in nature. They always lived close to a park and had space where they could grow food. It could be hard to find a safe, quiet, natural place to spend time in the city, so Willi's mother also took them to Ontario's "cottage country," where the kids could be near forests.

Throughout her youth, Willi explored her African roots and learned about Black Power and Black Pride, movements that

Willi with other Maroon grandmothers (descendents of Africans who escaped slavery). Maroon communities in Jamaica have been independent since a 1738–39 Peace and Friendship Treaty with the British. They have no taxes, no police and very little crime. *WILLI NOLAN-CAMPBELL*

helped Black people take a stand against the inequalities they faced in society. When she was 16, she learned that one of her grandmothers was Mi'kmaq (an Indigenous nation in Atlantic Canada). Later, she learned that one of her grandfathers was also Indigenous. When she started to explore that side of her heritage, she found a whole other set of struggles.

"I started to go to the library next to the Native Friendship Centre in Toronto and look for newspapers from Mi'kma'ki [the traditional territory of the Mi'kmaq Nation] to see what people were doing." They were calling on the government to lift them out of poverty, educating each other, sharing their traditional language and stories about respecting nature, and celebrating Indigenous people who had done great things.

When she was 19, Willi joined an organization that campaigned to stop the development of nuclear weapons. She went door-to-door to raise money on their behalf. The area where she did this happened to be one of the poorer areas of the city.

"Many people couldn't read or afford newspapers in that area. They didn't know what a nuclear weapon was," she says, but they were fascinated by what she had to say. "I was asked to come back. They wanted to know who was making these weapons and why, who they could speak to about it and what they could do." This information-sharing role would become central to Willi's life.

When Willi was expecting her second child, her doctor warned her about problems with the tap water in Toronto. What her doctor was saying was consistent with teachings she was receiving from Indigenous women, about what happens when people pollute and don't respect Mother Earth, and especially how it puts babies and pregnant women in danger. She started to research what was in the water she had been drinking and how she could find cleaner water.

That inspired her to start working with different groups to find or create alternatives to processes and products that caused pollution. She opened Green Clean, a clothes-cleaning business that used water instead of toxic dry-cleaning chemicals, and started Bio Business International, a company that marketed chlorine-free cotton tampons and environmentally friendly menstrual pads.

The world of business was not for Willi, however. She decided to move from the city with her children to a rural area

DID YOU KNOW?

When Willi's daughter was a baby, more than 30 years ago, it cost five dollars a jar to get organic baby food. Now, because there is greater awareness and a greater market for clean food, she can find it almost everywhere for less than a dollar.

Willi works with youth activists (including Morgan Curtis, right) to help get young people's voices heard at international climate change conferences. She says youth should realize their power and be wise. *GARRETT BLAD*

in Mi'kma'ki, where she could live her dream of being close to the wilderness full-time and be sure that they had clean food, air and water and a safe community.

Once there, Willi continued to work with the International Institute of Concern for Public Health, which was helping communities that were facing threats to their health because of environmental hazards. Under the guidance of medical scientist Dr. Rosalie Bertell, her job was to help those communities get medical, scientific and environmental information and support. She combined this information with Indigenous teachings. It was easy to translate between Indigenous and non-Indigenous experts, she remembers—again, everyone was saying the same thing, even if they said it in different ways.

After years of helping others, Willi's focus had to shift to her own rural community's environment. An energy company was planning something called ***hydraulic fracturing (fracking)*** in New Brunswick, where she lived. Fracking is a process of drilling into the earth and injecting a mixture of water, chemicals and sand at high pressure to release and collect the gas that's inside. Fracking uses a huge amount of water and can pollute underground water sources.

Willi's house was on the proposed frack line. So was her drinking water source. "It was an incoming disaster," she recalls.

That was the beginning of a journey Willi looks back on as both remarkable and punishing. "No matter how good an environmentalist I was before that, until I was fighting for my own water in my own community, I didn't really understand."

> "We have to have something in common and I always remember: we all drink water."

She began to experience firsthand how developers of massive projects can endanger the environment and more. "They threaten and violate people, they disrupt families, they set people one against the other. I learned about the systematic attempts to divide and conquer in communities."

Willi fought these divisive tactics with unity. She got information from doctors and scientists about how fracking could impact human and environmental health. Many people didn't know what fracking was, so for five years she took that information to local environmental groups and Indigenous communities. She called all the youth activists she knew and asked them to call their friends. One by one, people began to come together in the fight against fracking. From camping in the company's test sites to legal action, Indigenous and non-Indigenous protestors of all ages worked together.

"There were lawsuits, a massive public outcry and finally a complete regime change in government," Willi recalls.

A provincial election took place in the midst of the protests, and the people of New Brunswick elected an entirely new government.

Willi and others took demands voiced by youth and proposed text for a **moratorium** on fracking to the new government.

In 2016 the provincial government announced an indefinite moratorium on fracking. It later banned the disposal in New Brunswick of wastewater from fracking in other provinces and made plans to ban the burning of coal for energy.

"People forced the government to do the right thing. After consulting with doctors, lawyers, human rights experts, engineers, farmers, political scientists...I understood that no matter who we were, we had rights. If you take all of your rights and pool them together, you're going to box that government and corporation in until they leave you alone. Get an expert in scientific law, human rights lawyers, deluge them in all your rights. And then you win.

"I don't know how much money would have had to be raised to create the strength and duration of what we did," Willi reflects. "People brought what they could: poems, knitting, food, songs, connections, skills in writing press releases. We have a new economy building. You can't beat unity."

In the earlier days of Willi's work with environmental organizations, it wasn't common for people of different backgrounds to make efforts to understand how to work together. Over time, understanding how cultures are similar and how they are different, and gaining strength from bringing them together, has become an important part of her work and life.

> Willi says...
>
> **WHAT CAN YOU DO?**
> "Be the change. Find something in your community to do. Do it."

"I respect the cultures of my ancestors: the Mi'kmaq Nation of the Wabanaki, the Maroon people and the Welsh," Willi says. "I relish being of mixed blood. I've been working to find out the harmony of the original teachings, like respect for human life, animal life, the earth itself, the energies that we are and that we create. That's what I've been able to express in Mi'kmaq culture, Anishinaabe teachings, African teachings and Celtic teachings. The unanimity is that we have a Creator, the earth that's the Mother we're responsible for and to, and laws about love, kindness and respect. That trickles down to what I do, with the first step that I take. It trickles to the purchases I make and the thoughts I think. I'm working to keep that in any activism I do.

> "As I embrace the unity, the differences and the nuances of our relatives, they find a way to converge into one being, and that's me. You've got to work with what you've got."

"It has sustained me to know that these respectful teachings result in energy that transforms communities and people. Ways of changing can be very simple. I'm open to integrating the experiences of all my ancestors, predecessors, brothers and sisters who want to find a way for our earth and our peoples to have health and a good life."

Willi sets a pot of locally grown vegetables to simmer, then puts out a barrel to collect the rain that begins to fall outside her window. She says she's in really good health and she's at peace, which for her means success.

"I love this work."

Three

CLEANING UP THE MESS

Spreading Spores

DANIEL REYES

Scientist

Born in Monterrey, Mexico; lives in Austin, Texas

I'm a Mexican American man.

Daniel Reyes grew up in Monterrey, a large city in Mexico. There wasn't much to do inside, so he spent a lot of time outdoors playing sports and walking from home to school to football practice and back home again. Wherever he went, he was always curious. When he visited his abuela (grandmother), he'd follow his cousins down to the local creek.

Daniel's curiosity as a child helped him think outside the box as an adult.
COURTESY OF DANIEL REYES

These Monterrey creeks were a combination of open creek and paved storm sewer. While his cousins played with ants and did other wild kid things, Daniel stared at rocks and boulders, and skipped stones in the water. He brought his favorite rocks back to his grandma's house. One day, he wanted to get a snack from the store and thought of asking his aunts and uncles for some cash. But in the back of his mind, he could hear his mother's voice saying, "Never ask for money." He looked at his rock collection. If he loved the rocks so much, he thought, maybe others would too. So he bundled them into bags and sold them to his relatives to buy his snack.

One year Daniel's cousins traveled from southern Mexico to visit. He hadn't noticed before how stained and deformed their teeth were. "Why don't they brush their teeth?" he asked his mom. She told him they did, but that their city couldn't give them clean water. Daniel was shocked. They didn't have clean water? He couldn't imagine that someone in his own family didn't have something so basic, something he had taken for granted until that moment.

It stayed in the back of his mind until he went to college in Texas. When he had to choose a subject to focus on, he saw something called **hydrogeology**, the study of how water moves through rocks. That sounded good to him. For his final project, he looked at how the cleanliness of underground water sources can be affected as cities get bigger.

After Daniel graduated, he got a job on the emergency response team of an environmental consulting company that worked with oil and gas companies. One of his main tasks was to go to oil spills within the first 24 hours to measure how far they had spread, take samples and monitor the spills and their effects.

Daniel says...

WHAT CAN YOU DO?

"Be weird. Enjoy being the weird kid that you are. This curiosity you have and these weird things you like to do are important. Ask as many questions as you can. Be into things that other people aren't."

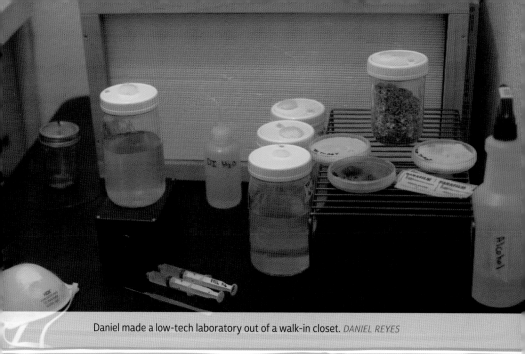

Daniel made a low-tech laboratory out of a walk-in closet. *DANIEL REYES*

"Doing that repeatedly over time," he remembers, "I was simply watching spill after spill taking the **contamination** from one place to another. Sometimes it would get cleaned up, sometimes it wouldn't."

Their job really wasn't to clean up the spills and all their ecological impacts. They could only do as much as their clients wanted. "And to me, that wasn't enough." Daniel had wanted a job that would be fulfilling. This wasn't it.

"I looked around for alternative solutions to cleaning up oil spills, and that's when I found fungi," he said.

As soon as he learned that fungi could break down oil, Daniel was hooked. He bought a bunch of scientific equipment, converted a walk-in closet in his home into a sterile lab and spent his spare time teaching himself about **mycology** (the study of fungi).

Putting himself back in that time, he's still amazed. "I was a hydrogeologist and now I'm looking at fungi. I'm watching **mycelium** grow on petri plates. I'm reading about experiments

Daniel's off-the-grid research station is set up in a contaminated site that's being converted into an ecological haven
COURTESY OF DANIEL REYES

and replicating them. I'm putting drops of diesel on these plates, watching the mycelium grow around it and reject the diesel for a day or two, and after that it consumes the diesel, completely breaks it down in a matter of two days. And I'm doing this for six months until I come home from an oil spill and I say, 'No more. That's it.' I went to my boss and quit my job."

Daniel told his boss he wanted to do something with fungi. She thought he was lying and was actually leaving to work for another consulting company. No matter what he said, she wouldn't believe what he was telling her.

Meanwhile, Daniel learned that an organization called the Amazon Mycorenewal Project was looking for volunteers to help use fungi to clean soil and water contaminated by oil drilling in the Amazon. He raised funds and bought a ticket to Ecuador to learn more about his new passion from experts. Or so he thought.

Daniel arrived in Ecuador and found himself surrounded not by experts but by other young international volunteers, all of whom were equally surprised. "After three days there, we looked around and said, 'Well, damn, this is it. This is the project. It's us.'" They had long discussions about what to do. Some people went home; Daniel and a few others stayed.

"I realized that a lot of the time, we look for experts to tell us what to do," Daniel says. "We expect that people already have the answers."

The experience made Daniel understand that people don't always have the answers. He thought about all the times he had heard people say that climate change or water problems are for someone else to worry about. He saw it as a sign that it was time for him and the other volunteers to take responsibility and develop the solutions themselves. The others agreed.

"That was a moment I'll never forget," he recalls. "I ended up staying for months, reworking the whole organization and its methods. We persevered and made that project our own."

Then Daniel brought that new experience back home to Austin, Texas. He partnered with an organization called Ecology Action that was trying to convert an area in a low-income neighborhood that had been a farm, then a quarry and finally a landfill into an ecological haven. They gave Daniel space to set up a research station where he could do experiments on how fungi can be used to clean polluted areas. The station is off the grid, using no running water or electricity; it collects rain water and has a composting toilet. In return for the space, he agreed to help them with public education projects. Community members young and old are learning new things from Daniel.

> *"I have this endless curiosity about the world and I'm passionate about sharing it. If I can't share it with one group of people because I don't speak the same language, I'm the first person to tell myself to learn that language and speak to them—or find someone else who can tell them."*

"The property is in one of the oldest neighborhoods in Austin, and it's totally overlooked by everybody else," he says. "They just remember it being a big dumpster and a burning landfill. We're changing people's perspectives on the land and on the role fungi play in our ecology.

"As I'm doing this, I'm diving deeper and deeper into this field that I thought I'd just learn about really quickly and apply. But now I find myself deep within the rabbit hole of fungi and mushrooms. And there's no escaping it," he says with a laugh. "My mission is to spread the spores: spread information on fungi and provide resources for those who need them."

Sometimes those who need them most, like people who live in the most polluted areas, are the least likely to have access— because either the information is too technical or they don't speak

Daniel gives lectures and classes in different languages to share what he's learning about the important role of fungi ecosystems and how people can grow and use them to improve their own living conditions. *COURTESY OF DANIEL REY*

English. Since Daniel can work in two languages—English and Spanish—he's able to reach many people.

Having people be able to both understand the results of research done by scientists and do their own research is very important to Daniel. He wants to pass his project along for the community to lead, because he thinks ordinary people can come up with great solutions to the world's problems if they're given the right information and tools. And young people can be the most creative of all.

"One time I was telling some kids about fungi that connect to the roots of plants and trees to exchange nutrients," he remembers. "One kid raises his hand and says, 'How does the plant know to interact with the fungus?' I got caught off guard." Daniel had never thought about that before. "And I thought, 'That's the thing that's going to make you an awesome scientist.' Because I'm saying the plant is alive, the fungus is alive, and the fungus attaches to the plant. And he says, 'Yeah, but how does it know?' Man…"

"Anybody can learn something and give a presentation. But when you break it down for someone, you get them involved, you get gloves on their hands and tell them, 'Mix this, feel it, smell it, taste it if you want'— that to me is most important."

DID YOU KNOW?

Mushrooms are only the visible part of a fungus. Most of the fungus is called *mycelium* and is hidden inside whatever it's growing in. Fungi reproduce by sending out spores, tiny units that can each create a new individual. There are up to five million species of fungi on earth, but we know fewer than 10 percent of them.

Clotilda Yakimchuk received the Order of Canada in 2003, one of the nation's highest honors, for her work to improve living conditions and promote education and for her leadership in health care. She also received the Queen Elizabeth II Diamond Jubilee Medal in 2012 and the Order of Nova Scotia in 2019.

COURTESY OF DR. CLOTILDA YAKIMCHUK

Preventing Cancer

DR. CLOTILDA YAKIMCHUK, CM

Community activist
**Born in Sydney, Cape Breton, Nova Scotia;
lives a few streets from where she was born**

*I'm one of four children born to Lillian and Arthur Coward
of the first generation of Barbadians that came to
Sydney, Nova Scotia, in 1917 to find employment.*

When Clotilda Yakimchuk was growing up in the 1930s and 1940s, her neighborhood of Whitney Pier in Sydney was cosmopolitan, with residents from the West Indies—mostly Barbados—as well as Jewish people, Italians and Hungarians. Her father had immigrated from Barbados to Nova Scotia to work in the local steel plant. But he faced discrimination there and was made to train a white person to get the promotion that he himself should have received. A proud Black man, he left the steel plant and started his own businesses delivering coal to homes and teaching music. These occupations filled a niche in the community, made him immune to the boom-and-bust nature of the steel industry and enabled him to feed his family in a healthy and traditional way.

Clotilda started her career when nursing schools in Nova Scotia were accepting very few Black students. She says, "Failures in life don't determine the road you will travel, because they are a part of life. People will sometimes turn down your requests, but don't let that be the end of the struggle." *DR. CLOTILDA YAKIMCHUK*

"In our household, there was always West Indian bread, rice and peas, chicken and *cou cou* on the table," Clotilda remembers. Her father's industriousness was characteristic of the people in her community, who made their livelihoods at the steel plant and in other jobs. "It was a very thriving, active community. It was beautiful growing up."

But Clotilda faced difficulties during her school years. She failed seventh grade because she was focusing on boys instead of school. When she brought home her report card, her father said, "Let this be a lesson to you. This is what happens when you don't apply yourself." Then in 11th grade, after her parents had separated, she wanted to quit school to work and help her mother make ends meet. Although her mother was working extra hard, she told her daughter, "No, no, no. We're having a hard time, but we'll get through. One of these days you may have to support your own children. Unless you have an education that will open doors for better employment, you won't be able to make it." So Clotilda focused, finished her schooling and decided to become a nurse.

Her mother's and father's perseverance and success in the face of discrimination and other challenges inspired Clotilda to be like them. In the 1950s nursing schools in Nova Scotia accepted few Black students. Clotilda became the first Black person admitted to the Nova Scotia Hospital School of Nursing in Dartmouth. She finished her diploma and married Benson Douglas, a Grenadian who had received his Masters of Law in the mid-1950s at Dalhousie University's law school. They left Nova Scotia and lived in Grenada for several years, where she studied midwifery. She returned to Canada to do post-graduate studies.

"One of the things I learned when I went to live in the West Indies," Clotilda recalls, "was that it was important for us as Black people to be active and speak out about issues of concern to us." While living in Grenada, she saw Black people in positions of power and leadership, something she hadn't seen back home in Cape Breton. And they asked questions when they felt things weren't right. "What I learned about the West Indies I tried to take back to Nova Scotia."

When she left Grenada and returned to Whitney Pier, she was shocked to see that the people of her largely Black community, which was adjacent to the steel plant, were living in poor conditions, including smoke-related air pollution and dilapidated housing. She thought, "This is not the way people should live."

The steel plant had been in operation for more than 100 years, and people in her community, many of whom worked at the plant, were getting sick with stomach and lung cancer. "Even with all the research done at the time, the federal, provincial and municipal

DID YOU KNOW?

Many people came from the West Indies, particularly Barbados, to Sydney, Nova Scotia, in the early part of the 20th century. They brought with them their food, music and organizations.

governments were reluctant to say it was because of the steel plant," Clotilda explains.

Remembering her experience in the West Indies, she started to speak out. Clotilda became a community activist, demanding improvements to her community's housing and living conditions. This included calling for the cleanup of the tar ponds that were by-products of making steel. The tar ponds were contaminating the houses so badly that many were scheduled to be torn down. The community was designated for a neighborhood improvement program to rebuild and revitalize people's homes. Although the area was still contaminated and no additional houses were supposed to be built in that area, the local mayor at the time had given permission for people to rebuild there anyway.

"I learned early that we should not just take, but that we should be concerned about the environment and the community around us. All of us can't be activists, but we can support some of the people who are quite active, because they need encouragement to continue."

Believing that their voices would be stronger as an organization rather than as individuals, Clotilda brought together like-minded people as the Black Community Development Organization (BCDO) of Cape Breton, with primary mandates of better housing and education, and promotion of Black culture. Clotilda was elected president.

Her mother had been right. When Clotilda's husband passed away, she was able to support their five children all by herself because of her nursing career. She became the director of the Cape Breton Regional Hospital's Education Services and was the only Black person in more than 100 years to be elected president of the Registered Nurses Association of Nova Scotia (now the College of Nurses).

While Clotilda was a child, civil rights leader Marcus Garvey (second from right) delivered a speech to the Black community in Sydney with words that would one day inspire Bob Marley: "We are going to emancipate ourselves from mental slavery...none but ourselves can free the mind." *MICHAEL OCHS ARCHIVES/GETTY IMAGES*

She later married Dan Yakimchuk, who had also worked at the steel plant and had begun attending BCDO meetings as a municipal councillor. They started working together on housing issues. The BCDO was successful in bringing new houses and better living conditions to the area.

Then a woman named Elizabeth May, who was the executive director of an environmental organization called the Sierra Club of Canada, began to host meetings in the area about the effects of the steel plant on the environment and on people's health. Clotilda and Dan went to those meetings. Elizabeth encouraged Clotilda

> Clotilda says...
>
> ### WHAT CAN YOU DO?
> "Ask questions. Don't be afraid to ask. If the answer is negative, don't let that be the end. Sometimes time can change things."

to become involved in the environmental aspects of the health crisis in her community. Elizabeth later encouraged her to join the board of directors of the Sierra Club of Canada.

At the time, it was rare to see a Black Canadian involved in the environmental movement. Clotilda thought that was strange, particularly given the environmentally related illnesses prevalent in her community. She began to question why others weren't involved and found that the concept of "environmental issues" was foreign to them. That disconnect inspired her to stay involved in the environmental movement, both as a link to her community and to address the root causes of their health problems.

"We continued to demand that the provincial government and then the federal government clean up the tar ponds," Clotilda says. Her campaigning took her to meetings with ministers of the environment from Canada, the United States and Mexico, to whom she explained what it was like to live in a contaminated community. It took her to a largely African American community in Atlanta, Georgia, that was also facing pollution from steel manufacturing. When she returned to Nova Scotia, she continued to organize protests, including a tent city set up outside the premier's house.

After about 10 years of campaigning by Clotilda and others, the governments finally agreed to devote money to the cleanup. It took many more years of remediation (cleaning up the pollution) before the cleanup of the tar ponds was considered to be completed. Where the tar ponds were is now a picturesque park

DID YOU KNOW?

The cleanup of the Sydney tar ponds is among the most prominent *remediation* projects in Canada.

DID YOU KNOW?

West Indian women brought a community microcredit practice known as susu to Cape Breton. It is a savings system in which each participant contributes a modest amount each week, and each week one of the participants receives the entire sum of money. This practice is still common in West Africa, which is an ancestral place of origin of many West Indian people.

with trees, flowers and benches, where people can sit and enjoy their surroundings.

Clotilda's parents had taught her that failure meant you learned and rose up again. This kept her going during her work on the Sydney tar ponds. Her activities weren't always immediately successful. She and the people she worked with had to repeatedly rethink and reevaluate their goals and strategies, trying different things to achieve what they wanted.

Although change doesn't happen quickly, she says, we need to keep pushing for the improvements we want to see. Clotilda encourages people to look at their communities' needs and contribute however they can. She feels it's important that we all speak up, question things we believe may be wrong and, if we don't get the right answers, keep asking.

Perseverance is key, she says. "I still use it now. I'm still involved in activities in my community. Not always have I been successful in the beginning, but you sit down, you pause, you look again at what you have been doing, look at the progress or lack of progress, and then you keep going. Don't accept a no."

Richelle Kahui-McConnell weaves holes in mesh "socks" with harakeke (flax) to deploy taura (rope) on which mussels will be grown to filter out urban pollution in one of Auckland's bays. *CHARLOTTE GRAHAM*

Restoring
Ancestral Waters

RICHELLE KAHUI-McCONNELL

Kaiwhakaora Whenua (Earth Healer) and former nurse
Born in a small forestry town called Tokoroa, Waikato; grew up and lives in Auckland, New Zealand

As Māori, our whakapapa (lineage) is to Papatūānuku (Mother Earth). Generations of all beings, including humans, are part of the ecosystem, which is why we call ourselves Tangata Whenua (People of the Earth).

ko Tainui te waka, ko Pirongia te maunga, ko Maungapu te awa, ko Maniapoto te iwi, ko Huiao raua Kinohaku nga hapū, ko Rereamanu raua Te Kauae nga marae, te Rauna Hauangi Kahui Tangaroa taku koroua

This introduces the waka (canoe) we came over on from Hawaiki (ancestral homeland), my mountain, my river, my hapū (tribe) and my marae (meeting house). We were created from the earth.

I t is said that Māori voyagers traveled from Hawaiki to Aotearoa 600 to 1,000 years ago. They are kaitiaki (stewards) of the islands and their waters. After Europeans colonized Aotearoa and called it New Zealand, everything changed. Māori lost a lot of their land, their culture and their lives. Wars and new diseases made their population fall to a fraction of what it

Richelle learned to be proud of who she is, who she comes from and her connection and responsibility to the earth.
NINA STOWERS

once was. Urban sprawl and industrial development began. Richelle Kahui-McConnell's family, like many others, was forced to move from their homeland to the city.

Richelle remembers being a young girl in Auckland, swimming in a river that flowed to the beach. Years later, she learned that it wasn't a river at all—it was a stormwater drain. It had been carrying pollutants—and sometimes sewage—from Auckland, New Zealand's biggest city, across the beach and into the ocean for 100 years.

Other than that urban beach, Richelle didn't grow up with much connection to nature or her cultures—Māori on her father's

Richelle's mentor, Kaumatua Tamaiti Tamaariki, lays down mussels to help clean his ancestral bay. *CHARLOTTE GRAHAM*

side and Samoan on her mother's. Her family never went camping, on bush walks or to their ancestral mountain or river.

Richelle was gifted as a healer, so she became an HIV nurse. This was in the 1990s, when **antiretroviral** medicines were harder to get, and many of her patients died. It was very hard on her, and after several years she was burnt out.

She decided to go into the bush, where she found that her healing skills were needed just as much. Then she returned to the city to do an environmental degree, with a focus on **conservation management** and **restoration ecology**. As soon as she went into nature with her class, she felt that she'd made the right choice. She heard the voices of her ancestors telling her that she was where she needed to be, that it was her life's path to address the injustices that had been done.

> "When I walk into a room as an environmental scientist, I have all my ancestors standing behind me. I have this beautiful assurance that somebody's got my back and I'm never on my own. I feel like I'm channeling messages from them, tikanga—the right things to do."

"I wanted to be there forever and have that feeling around me. Our health is a reflection of the health of our land. You have to understand where our illness comes from, and it's from the earth."

After years of standing up for their rights, Māori got to be involved in governing and managing the country. People were finally starting to listen to them. They had laid the path for people like Richelle to bring the voices of the ancestors to the table to work with the government to make decisions for the benefit of future generations. Since then, everything Richelle has done has been for the protection and restoration of Papatūānuku and mauri (life force).

"We have something called kaitiakitanga (**stewardship**). Because we are created from the earth, our obligation is to protect

The joyous day when Richelle and the Māori Iwi deposited 2.2 tons (2 tonnes) of mussels into the water off their waka (canoes), reestablishing their connection with the bay. *CHARLOTTE GRAHAM*

everything else that is part of that ecosystem. We're just a part of it; we're not above it."

After finishing her degree, Richelle recalled her only nature-related childhood memory: being on that beach in Auckland with her whānau (family), harvesting pipi (a bivalve shellfish), cooking it right there and tasting its salty goodness out of her sandy little hands. During the 40 years that had passed, so many changes had happened in Auckland that the bivalves either became too contaminated to eat or had disappeared entirely.

Richelle went to the Māori Iwi (community) within whose territory that beach was and asked them how she could help. For 150 years they had been trying to protect the mauri of the bay where that beach was. For 30 years they had tried to tell the government that their shellfish were dying and their people were dying, that they had faced diseases like cholera and typhoid because of the sewage. Nobody was listening to them.

"It decreased their mana (strength and power), because people were dying when they visited. The hapū (tribe) lost connection with their ancestral bay because they weren't expressing their cultural practices, and when they were, they got sick," Richelle says. "The bay itself was really sick. Over the years, children had been told not to swim in it."

Using Richelle's scientific training and the community's mātauranga (Māori *Traditional Knowledge*), they defined *indicators* of cultural health based on mauri. They first defined a healthy bay as one where they wouldn't hesitate to walk into the water.

Using those waters had been a central part of their lives since their ancestors first arrived on Aotearoa. For them to hesitate before walking in showed that something had really gone wrong. So that was the first indicator.

The second indicator they defined was being able to harvest seafood, which hadn't been possible for decades because of pollution being flushed into the bay.

Richelle and the Iwi started monitoring for shellfish in the bay and found almost none. Then they studied what was in the bay's *sediments* and found heavy metals and other toxins. It confirmed in Western scientific terms what the community had already known for decades through their mātauranga.

By combining Western and Māori worldviews, Richelle can speak about the same issues to New Zealand's Environment Court using Western scientific terms and to Elders in a marae (meeting house) using Māori terms. She's been able to translate from one group to the other, which has helped them understand each other better.

They used all their knowledge to create a restoration plan for the bay and began to take action. This included separating sewage from stormwater, opening streams that had been pushed into pipes, using mussels to filter toxins out of the water, and stopping the practice of removing washed-up seaweed on the beaches that birds and other animals need as food.

The next challenge was to convince the city to move 250 moored boats—owned by wealthy people—that had been in the bay for many years and were leaching copper into the water.

Families knew that the water in the bay wasn't circulating and flushing like it used to before the shorelines were modified for the city and that they couldn't swim in it like their grandparents used to.

Richelle and the Iwi worked with leading universities to study the sediments in the bay. "We found that everything was settling underneath the boats. Under the moorings where the boats were, the copper was twice as high as where the boats weren't. Combined with whānau saying, 'It affects our mauri because we can't be ourselves in our bay,' we had enough of a case for the Environment Court to agree to shift the moorings out of the bay. That was huge.

"Ten years ago, the fish weren't in the bay. The birds weren't there," Richelle recalls. "When you sit in the bay now and the tide recedes, you can see that the seagrass has started to return and

Richelle says...

WHAT CAN YOU DO?

"Pick up a piece of rubbish! Say no to plastic. Say no to unethical products. Don't buy cheap plastic things that just break. Question where something comes from: What happened? How did we get it?"

One of the achievements Richelle (bottom left) is most proud of is helping facilitate the first rangatahi (youth) climate change summit in Aotearoa's largest city. The rangatahi will be writing a youth climate change action plan. *KAHURANGI RATANA-WILSON*

there is wildlife throughout the bay. The bird-life is phenomenal."

What Richelle is most proud of, though, is helping whānau reconnect with their bay. She created programs for schools in the area, special learning spaces, internships and scholarships for youth. She took young people into nature to learn about science and see the difference between healthy and unhealthy environments. She had kids hold soil in their hands, crumble it, smell it and think about its mauri, then look at it under a microscope to see how it compared with what they had sensed. Youth ran the shellfish-monitoring program for five years, inspiring Richelle to create a young environmental leaders program.

"We asked our youth, 'How do you feel when we are swimming in the ocean? How do you feel when we're walking through

> *"We talk about knowledge not being ours. It's our duty to share knowledge. It's our duty to bring the wider community around us. If we separate ourselves, how can anybody understand how to be on our journey with us?"*

the bush and one of our birds comes and flits around your feet?' They can talk about that feeling for hours. Then we talked about how to bring that to youth who have never been to the ocean, or who don't go to the bush."

Richelle saw that the only way to involve kids was to recognize how intelligent they are, talk to them with respect and show them the beauty of the world. "I didn't have that wondrous connection as a child, to feel what it's like to be in nature. So to be a protector now means to me that there's great potential for every child," she says.

"The coolest part of this work is getting whānau into boats, dropping off the mussels, tasting their own mussels and then saying, 'I want to protect them.' They come down now and ask, 'How are *our* mussels growing?' They have ownership of the project. It's not only the physical restoration; it's that ultimate movement of the people."

DID YOU KNOW?

Richelle has done all this work as an independent individual. She collaborates and co-designs *holistic* projects with a collective of friends who are economists, ecologists and accountants, because restoring mauri means restoring environmental, social and economic well-being.

Richelle on Ōkahu Bay with taura in her hands. The rope was used by Māori in the past to grow mussels for eating. It has been adopted again to enable whānau (family) to clean an urban bay and restore this ancient and vital practice and food source. *JESSICA KATE TWEED*

HILLARY BEATTIE

Four

RESPECTING WISDOM

Ghanimat Azhdari with young Baluch girls in their territory in the southeast part of Iran. Ghanimat's organization has helped map the Baluch Tribal Confederacy's territory. *GHANIMAT AZHDARI/CENESTA*

Mapping Knowledge

GHANIMAT AZHDARI

*Participatory mapping and natural resources conservation
and management expert*
Born in Shiraz, Iran

I'm an Indigenous tribal girl.

Imagine waking up every day in your family's tent, looking out to see your sheep and goats grazing on the meadow, with a great mountain in the distance. You fetch water to drink from a spring that your family has maintained since before the time of your great-grandparents. Nature around you is vast, but you know the name and use of every plant. In your culture, it's forbidden to cut down a tree except in emergencies and even then only in a way that will make sure the other trees survive. When your paths cross those of others, you speak of your extended families and communities and trace your connections with each other. This is the way of life of Ghanimat Azhdari's nomadic Qashqai people.

Ever since she was a child, Ghanimat Azhdari felt a strong bond with her tribe because of their connection to the land and to their animals.
COURTESY OF GHANIMAT AZHDARI

Ghanimat is identifying rangeland plants and recording their locations. The diverse plants of Iran's rangelands have evolved alongside pastoralists. Ghanimat's people and other Indigenous nomadic pastoralists have been conservin their territories for thousands of years. By migrating, they don't use up the natural resources they depend on. *CENES*

Ghanimat was born and raised in a big city, but whenever she visited her relatives and tribespeople in their territory on *pastoral* lands, on a migration route that has sustained them for generations, she felt calm and secure, more than she ever felt anywhere else. She wished she could stay on those lands forever. Their natural environment was what she loved the most.

"My tribe and my tribal confederacy are so connected with nature," she explains. "We never want to destroy anything. It is a two-way connection: we are taking care of nature, and nature is giving us its blessing."

She kept having to return to the city, where her parents lived, but she made the most of her life there by getting degrees in

DID YOU KNOW?

According to official figures, Indigenous nomadic tribes use 59 percent of the land in Iran.

natural resources and rangeland management, with the goal of being able to do something for her tribe and their lands.

"I started to work for the government in the Natural Resources office in a small town close to the territory of my tribe. I was the officer of rangeland issues in that region. I was working on different projects connected with Indigenous Peoples and the nomadic pastoralist people."

What she didn't expect were the conflicts between her tribe and the government office. Qashqai people, like other nomadic people in Iran, migrate with their livestock between summering and wintering grounds. It's a difficult journey, and one they have taken for generations based on their intimate knowledge of all the natural elements that they and their animals need, from plants to wildlife to weather.

One of their conflicts was when the government told them they had to migrate on a particular date. But the Qashqai people knew that the date chosen by the government was at a time of year that wouldn't be good for the plants, people or animals.

> "We have a lot of unity in our community. We are individuals, but we are in a group, so we have pride and we have power. This, in all the communities, should flourish because people want to know that they are not alone, that they are a very powerful group."

Ghanimat understood that the community knew best when they should and shouldn't migrate. She tried to intervene, but her bosses and colleagues didn't appreciate her dedication to her people, her closeness to the environmental issues that affected them, or her defense of their expert knowledge when it wasn't consistent with government policies.

"You want to help them all the time, because they are your tribesmen," her supervisors told her. "You should act according to official regulations, not your emotions."

She was also learning how much of her tribe's territory, the beautiful landscapes she had visited since her childhood, was being damaged by things like construction and changes in the climate. She began to feel very sad. After three years, she saw that working for the government wouldn't let her accomplish her goals. She quit and became a university lecturer, hoping that transferring her knowledge to young people would help her community. Even then, she still wasn't able to do what she felt she needed to do.

Then Ghanimat learned that Cenesta (Centre for Sustainable Development and Environment), the oldest nonprofit civil society organization in Iran, was working on Indigenous Peoples' rights. "This was what I was really interested in," she remembers. She took a job there.

Having grown up around nomadic people, she had seen how well they knew the geographical and ecological details of their lands, but all that information was in their brains and in their ways of life. Meanwhile, the government made its decisions using maps that didn't accurately depict nomadic peoples' territories or reflect their knowledge.

Ghanimat saw the power her people could have if they were able to translate their knowledge into a format that government officials would understand. "If they had their own map in their

Ghanimat says...

WHAT CAN YOU DO?

"Learn to identify a *native plant* in your area and to identify an *invasive plant* that can destroy the native plant. Take care of the native plant. It's like a friendship. If new people come into your life, you still need to take care of those who have been there all the time, so that you don't lose them."

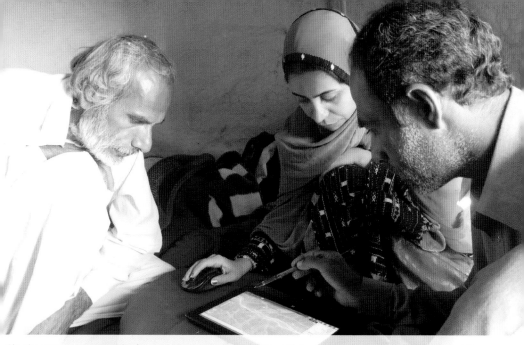

Ghanimat saw an opportunity for nomadic pastoralists to protect their migration routes and the plants that they and their livestock depend on by translating their knowledge of the land onto maps. In this photo she is doing participatory mapping with a Baluch community in their territory. *GHANIMAT AZHDARI/CENESTA*

hands, they could go to the different government offices and say, 'This is our territory and we have rights on our ancestral territory.'"

So Ghanimat started participatory mapping, which is exactly what it sounds like: people gather around and participate in making a map by sharing their knowledge. Many of the people she was working with couldn't read or write and had never used paper maps. Ghanimat's knowledge of mapping, on the other hand, had been very technical—she had never used it in a participatory setting before. So they all learned by doing.

The communities that had never worked with maps started by sketching details on a piece of paper. These included the features that marked territorial borders, summering and wintering grounds, migration routes, special points along those routes and important areas for wildlife. They recorded the plants they conserve and use for medicine, feeding livestock and

Ghanimat starts participatory mapping with communities by working with them to transfer their knowledge of the landscape and ecosystems to paper maps. Here she is working with Indigenous women in the Abolhasani Tribal Confederacy's territory near the central desert of Iran. *GHANIMAT AZHDARI/CENESTA*

other purposes. They also noted where factories, oil and gas companies, and developers had invaded the territories.

From their own sketch maps, they moved to marking up official maps that showed the topography of the land, then to online maps using Google Earth, and afterward to geographic information systems—specialized computer software used to analyze all sorts of information related to the maps. Within four years, 55 different tribes had mapped their territories with the help of Ghanimat and Cenesta. They started talking with government officials to try to make the official maps depict their territories more accurately.

"This is something that always makes me happy," Ghanimat says, the joy flowing from her words. "Even if these community maps are not accepted by the government now, after five or ten years they are something that will empower the communities. Because they have maps in their hands, they can advocate for their territories."

Ghanimat has been able to exercise her passion by working with Cenesta, including representing them in an international organization that works with Indigenous Peoples and conservation. If she gets a call for help from a tribe, she goes above and beyond her job duties to mobilize support for them, because she sees their problems as her own and knows that she is their link to and voice in the wider world. She also uses her international work to spread good news about Iran, which gets a lot of negative media attention that is sometimes based on incorrect information.

> "It is important for young people to never forget what they had before. Their ancestors experienced many things and learned things after many years. If we forget these things because we want to gain something new, we are losing everything we have."

After creating paper maps, Ghanimat and the people in the communities she works with move on to developing maps using computer software. Here she is delineating Bakhtiari communities' territorial map.
GHANIMAT AZHDARI/CENESTA

Ghanimat is the youngest member of the Council of the ICCA Consortium, an international organization that promotes the recognition and support of ICCAs (Indigenous Peoples' and Community Conserved Areas and Territories). This photo was taken when she was at the Conference of the Parties to the Convention on Biological Diversity in Mexico in 2016. *COURTESY OF GHANIMAT AZHDARI*

Being part of a national and international movement has given Ghanimat hope that she spreads to her people back home, who often feel like they can't speak up for their rights and the health of their territories. She tells them, "We should be so powerful because many people in the world are thinking about us and thinking about you. We can make change in the world."

Ghanimat with her two main mentors: her great, beloved teacher Dr. M. Taghi Farvar (right), former ICCA Consortium president and former chair of Cenesta, and her role model, Dr. Grazia Borrini-Feyerabend (left), ICCA Consortium global coordinator. *GHANIMAT AZHDARI/CENESTA*

Preserving Forest-People Relationships

KENDI BORONA

Lecturer in human dimensions of conservation
Born in Meru, Kenya; lives in Kimana, Kenya

I identify myself first as an African and second as a Kenyan.
Thirdly, I'm a Mumeru woman.

When Kendi Borona was five years old, she went with other women in her family to collect water and bring it back to her village in rural Kenya. The water was heavy and they were on foot. She lagged behind and her aunties called back to her, saying, "You have to catch up, you have to do this." At that moment, she became worried about how difficult her life was going to be if that was what she was expected to do.

But Kendi was lucky. Not long after that, water was piped to her village from a source in their local forest and she no longer had to fetch it. Instead, she had the opportunity to

Kendi at about six years old at her family home.
COURTESY OF KENDI BORONA

spend her time getting an education and exploring things she was interested in.

"Water is a game-changer for any woman in Africa," she says. "If you have to spend time getting water, you don't have time for anything else, including education."

Watersheds are large areas of land where all the water drains and collects in the same place. The reason why Kendi's community was able to get piped water was that their local forest and the watersheds it contained were protected by an Indigenous custodial system. The forest contains sacred places where community Elders go for prayers. Some areas are so sacred that the community only lets certain people enter them.

"Indigenous knowledge protected those watersheds," she explains, "providing water for people like me who were living downstream."

The knowledge that a forest protected by her community saved her from a life of water-gathering sparked Kendi's interest in conservation and the role that communities play in it. But even when she studied conservation in university, she wasn't taught that communities themselves might have knowledge or cultural values that could help the cause. She and her fellow students were led to believe that communities had to be taught how to be conservation-minded.

Kendi says...

WHAT CAN YOU DO?

"Study your history. Understand problems faced by placing them within a historical context. Try to understand the root causes, then make a contribution to that issue."

Kendi picks coffee while doing her research in central Kenya. *COURTESY OF KENDI BORONA*

"We have been 'de-cultured,'" she says. "We have been taught that the way to be civilized is to strip yourself of any Indigenous value systems. But people have been living in landscapes for generations and creating knowledge based on these landscapes."

Kendi's direct connection with the land, and the benefits she herself had experienced from healthy ecosystems and communities, inspired her to understand and work on the connection between communities and the environment.

"Historically," she explains, "conservation has been seen as creating pristine protected areas without community involvement or by locking communities out of their landscapes." When that

DID YOU KNOW?

Kenyan forests exist on land that historically belongs to communities.

happens, communities feel burdened by conservation and don't experience its benefits. Kendi wanted to put communities back into the picture, for ecosystem health and for social justice. "I think conservation is more robust when it's responding to the needs, livelihoods and interests of people who live within the land-scapes."

> "Communicate effectively and consistently, and try to engage as many people as possible."

She took a job with an organization called the Trust for African Rock Art. For that job, she worked in Kenya, Uganda, Tanzania and Malawi over eight years to protect cultural landscapes. Her projects started small, with the conservation of sites that contained paintings and engravings on stone. "I was responsible for working with communities to figure out how we can promote this heritage,

Kendi held a talking-circle meeting with communities living at the edge of the forest. Working with local communities and their knowledge is essential to conservation—people are part of the picture. *KENDI BORONA*

create awareness of it and generate revenue from these sites to improve their livelihoods."

Those rock art sites were just one aspect of the environment that was significant to local people. The sites were located within a **biodiverse** area that included mountains, trees and other habitats, as well as Indigenous foods. By working closely with the communities, Kendi contributed to the growth of the project bit by bit to include the development of a cultural center, reforestation programs, and revitalization of plants and heritage varieties of foods. One of these communities was the Iteso people of western Kenya. Through the project, they created the annual Iteso cultural festival, which has brought together 10,000 people from Uganda and Kenya to revitalize Indigenous practices.

"If you really want to change something, you're going to change it not by sitting in high-powered meetings but by engaging with that woman who is going to fetch firewood or that man who is going to hunt an animal—through a dialogue with people who are living on the land."

The more Kendi worked directly with local people, the more conscious she became of how their cultures linked with conservation. That made her even more interested in her own culture and other African Indigenous knowledge systems that support both conservation and people's livelihoods, two things that are closely linked.

DID YOU KNOW?
There are more than ten major forested landscapes in Kenya. They all support the Kenyan economy and community livelihoods.

She began to study the work of Nobel Laureate Wangari Maathai, who is also from Kenya. Professor Maathai argued that revitalizing Africa's cultural heritage and putting it in the center of environmental discussions can restore people's dignity, landscapes and livelihoods. During her PhD program, Kendi worked with the women who restore forests as part of the Green Belt Movement, an organization founded by Professor Maathai.

> **DID YOU KNOW?**
> More than 90 percent of water in Kenya comes from forested landscapes.

Kendi has experienced firsthand what happens when authorities make decisions based on local knowledge and what happens when they don't. "I grew up based on the land. I know what it means to be without water. That's a very serious issue. If you have deforested everything or if you have planted tree species that cannot provide good fuel, that spirals into so many other directions.

"I am a beneficiary not just of the forest but of Indigenous knowledge systems that protect critical watersheds that protect the land," Kendi says. "That's why I now study Indigenous knowledge systems and conservation."

> **DID YOU KNOW?**
> Many of Kenya's forests have survived because of the struggle led by Wangari Maathai and other like-minded Kenyans against forest destruction that had been sanctioned by the Kenyan government in the 1990s.

Kendi plants a tree at the edge of the Nyandarwa forest in Kenya. She studied people's relationships with that forest and how their Indigenous knowledge could contribute to conservation and sustainability as Kenya's social, economic and political situation changes. *COURTESY OF KENDI BORONA*

Understanding Fisheries

SAUL BROWN, 'HAZIL'HBA

*Heiltsuk Haiłcístut (Reconciliation) negotiator and
student of Heiltsuk culture, laws and governance*
**Born in unceded Tsleil-Waututh, Squamish and Musqueam
territory; lives in the community of Wáglísla in Heiltsuk territory**

*I come from the House of Dhadhiyasila on my Heiltsuk side
and from the Little, Robinson and Thomas families on the
Nuu-chah-nulth side. Everything with my identity ties back to who
I am as an Indigenous person. I have three beautiful Indigenous
sisters. I'm Frank and Kathy Brown's son, Jimmy and Margaret
Brown's grandson, Luke and Elsie Robinson's grandson. I honor the
brilliance of my ancestors in the face of the colonial legacy.*

Back in the days when supernatural beings roamed the earth alongside humans, Raven wanted more herring. He filled his canoe and then tipped it to spread that little fish from one area to another, increasing its abundance. That central act in the Heiltsuk people's history taught them how to manage their relationship with herring and increase its abundance, and shows how important it is to their way of life. The Heiltsuk developed a tradition of placing kelp fronds and tree branches into the water for herring to spawn on, harvesting the kelp and branches with eggs on them and letting the herring live to spawn again.

Saul with his great granny Maggie Hall (Humchitt).
FRANK BROWN

Thousands of years later, settlers created the colonial state of Canada and imposed it on the territories of West Coast Indigenous Peoples. It created a Department of Marine and Fisheries (now known as Fisheries and Oceans Canada, or DFO) in 1867. Canada began to sell commercial fishing licenses and limited how Indigenous Peoples could fish. The government wouldn't let them sell their catch, even though trading fish for other goods had always been an important part of their lives.

Japan started to buy herring, and commercial herring fishing in Pacific Canada grew so much that the fishery became unsustainable and collapsed. After a while, the fish populations increased a bit and some countries wanted to buy herring eggs. The Canadian commercial fishery caught the herring before they spawned and killed them to take out their eggs. Meanwhile, Indigenous Peoples still fought for their rights to harvest herring sustainably and sell their catch. In 1988 two Heiltsuk brothers

Saul says...

WHAT CAN YOU DO?

"Find out whose Indigenous territory you live on. Find out what the landscape looked like before colonization. And get outside and play in the environment, so you can start to value it."

were arrested and charged with selling herring spawn (eggs) on kelp without a license.

Saul Brown hadn't even been born yet, but his path was being set. In 1996, those brothers won their case at the highest court in Canada. Still, the Heiltsuk's fight continued.

As an eight-year-old, Saul remembers being on his family's fishing boat, making sandwiches and laughing at jokes. Their boat and others from the community stopped near an 80-foot seine boat run by a commercial fishing company. The people on the seiner, including DFO officers armed with assault rifles, started yelling racial insults over the radio. In response, the Heiltsuk sang their traditional songs over the radio. As the insults got worse, the Heiltsuk sang louder. A few people, including Saul's feisty Auntie Harriet and many community Chiefs, got from their boats into a traditional oceangoing canoe. Someone put Saul into the canoe too. Still singing, they paddled into the middle of the seine net that was going to close around many tons of herring. Auntie Harriet started splashing water on the seiner with her paddle. The Heiltsuk on the other boats threw firecrackers into the water to scare the herring away from the net.

Saul with his grandma Elsie Robinson. *FRANK BROWN*

"I was really frightened," Saul remembers, "seeing our canoe built from a cedar log next to this massive aluminum seiner. But it galvanized me to think, 'This is who I am and this is my responsibility.'"

He knew his community was out there not because of hatred but because of love for their people and the herring. The seiner was about to kill hundreds of thousands of herring at a time when the Heiltsuk knew there weren't enough to support that kind of fishery. That event shaped Saul's future.

DID YOU KNOW?
A school of herring can be several miles long.

"Herring is an issue I'm working on now, that I was working on, that I'll probably grow old working on and die working on," he tells me.

Scientists have since begun to call herring a **keystone species**, one that is connected with so many parts of the food web that what affects it can affect pretty much everything else. But the Heiltsuk and other coastal Indigenous Peoples had always known this.

"For us, everything begins with the herring," Saul explains. "When they come, it's the beginning of our new year. They're woven into our whole culture, our whole identity."

In March 2015, herring were arriving near the shores of Wáglísla (Bella Bella). Their numbers had been so low for six years that some of Saul's nieces and nephews had never eaten herring eggs. Saul was near the end of his semester at the University of Victoria. "I got a phone call from my dad, who said, 'I'm tired, and I'm afraid they're going to open the fishery.' He sounded really deflated. I've never known my father to be wounded to the point where he didn't have any fight left in him."

Saul's father, a strong voice for the community, knew that the herring needed more time to recover; opening the commercial fishery would devastate them. He was reaching out to his son for help. So Saul said, "I'm not going to let being in a colonial institution pacify me as a Heiltsuk person."

Saul got the first ferry home, a journey that took him a whole day and night. "I didn't know what was going to happen—if I was going to fail all my classes—but I emailed my professors and told them what I was doing."

In Bella Bella he joined a meeting of a dozen community members, none of whom seemed very passionate. "I got this feeling that our whole community was deflated from constantly having to go to court, constantly having to fight to protect our commercial Aboriginal rights, our relationship with herring, the knowledge, the intergenerational teachings, our food security, all these things that the herring give us."

With Saul's encouragement, they made a plan for a nonviolent protest. They filled a canoe with mostly women and children, paddled to the DFO office and gave it a notice of eviction from their territory. But as they were getting ready to leave, Saul stopped.

"We can't serve an eviction notice to a wrongly erected building in our territory and just walk away," he told the others. "Because then what's the use? It's just an empty threat. I'm not leaving."

The elected Heiltsuk leaders agreed; they had just had unsuccessful meetings with the Canadian government. So about 50 Heiltsuk community members entered the building that housed the DFO office. They saw a DFO officer and told him, "We know this isn't your doing, but it's the minister and her advisors in

DID YOU KNOW?

Animals that eat herring or their eggs include whales, seals, sea lions, fish, seabirds, shorebirds, eagles, land animals such as bears, wolves and humans, and invertebrates such as sea stars, crabs and shrimp.

Ottawa who are keeping this fishery open. You know that if you fish, you're going to deplete the stocks again. This is madness. We value you, but we're not going to leave."

The Heiltsuk Chief Councillor and another leader had been invited into the office for a meeting, and they intended to stay there in protest. The other community members had planned to push their way in but were blocked by the police. They stayed outside, and the leaders stayed inside, for several days and nights, singing their traditional herring song and insisting that the fishery be called off.

They knew that their small, isolated village wouldn't get enough attention on its own. So while they were staging their sit-in protest, they contacted their family members and allies in

Saul Brown and his family harvesting hán̓t (herring roe on hemlock), a traditional practice that doesn't kill the spawning fish. *DEIRDRE LEOWINATA*

the bigger cities of Vancouver and Victoria. Most of the commercial herring licenses on the Canadian West Coast are owned or controlled by a company that also owns a major grocery chain. That company even supplies food to Bella Bella. People protested at the fishery company and occupied DFO offices in downtown Vancouver. In Victoria, protesters blocked a shopping center containing one of the chain's grocery stores. They faced unexpected rage; one of Saul's schoolmates in Victoria was punched in the stomach by an angry shopper.

> **DID YOU KNOW?**
> Saul didn't fail his university classes after he left for Bella Bella. He did well.

All those actions got the issue into the news and social media, and the Heiltsuk got the attention they needed.

DFO's test fisheries confirmed that there weren't enough fish for the commercial fishery to be successful. They called it off and began working on an agreement with the Heiltsuk, describing their commercial Aboriginal rights to harvest.

"It was a beautiful thing to see what happens when law meets law," Saul recalls. "Our Ǵvíḷás, our ancient laws, dictated that we stand up for the herring. The whole ecosystem and the Heiltsuk need the herring to come back. And Canadian laws sanctioned that."

In the following two years, herring were abundant in Heiltsuk territory. Saul thinks that protecting their physical numbers was one reason why, but that there was more to it.

"There's also a spiritual aspect," Saul explains. "We stood up for the herring, and they came back in record numbers. I believe that when we engaged in the deep relationship our ancestors engaged in, the herring were looking out for us."

For abundance like this to continue, Saul sees that Indigenous Peoples need space and power to govern their own territories, communities and families and to be respected as nations.

Saul on the water during the 2018 herring season in Heiltsuk territory. His work and culture take him outdoors and let him gain a deep understanding of and appreciation for nature. *ADRIAN SAMARRA*

They know best how to heal their people and their environment. Every island, species and stretch of water in their territory has meaning for them. They have developed those relationships over hundreds of generations.

Saul says that when you're in nature, bathing in it and thanking it for what it provides, you learn to value it. When your life takes you outdoors, the weather, tides and wind control you and become part of you. After his initiation at a Potlatch, Saul's family gave him the name 'Hazil'hba, which ties him to a specific place within Heiltsuk territory. If it's ever in danger, he has to go and protect it.

"Our old people say this is your duty as a Heiltsuk person, to stand up," Saul explains. "It's not just someone saying this is the most ethical thing to do. It's not debated, it's told. We don't wonder, 'What is my meaning in life?' We know this is our duty and this is our meaning."

"For the Indigenous kid: Don't accept the anthropologist who's an 'expert' on your culture. Don't accept the linguist who tells you how your language is supposed to be spoken. Don't accept the stereotypes that the world projects onto you. Stay true to you, stay true to your teachings, stay true to your Elders and be fearless in that. Because you're powerful. You come from a very powerful place, and very powerful people. If you're humble enough and you have enough gratitude, that power will flow through you if you allow it."

CURTIS ANDREWS

Five

SAVING THE ANIMALS

Dipani works with communities and students around the coasts of India to study marine mammals.
COURTESY OF DIPANI SUTARIA

Discovering Dolphins

DIPANI SUTARIA

Freelance ecologist
Born and lives in Ahmedabad, India

*I identify as a woman first, then a researcher and an environmental
protector and everything else that comes along with it.*

"I grew up with a pet," Dipani Sutaria recounts, "which is something I can never thank my parents enough for."
Dipani's dog, Champ, made her connect with the outdoors when she was a kid. "He wanted to be out," she remembers. "And I wanted to be out with him." Champ found crows irritating. So Dipani didn't let them take any of his chapatis (flatbreads). But he didn't mind sharing with a different bird called a bulbul. One bulbul let Dipani get close enough that when she went home she was able to draw his picture from memory. Then she started taking photos of him—and of other animals. She didn't realize at the time how important that new hobby would be to her life's work.

Dipani with her sister and their dog, Champ, in Ahmedabad, Gujarat, about 300 miles (500 kilometers) from the sea.
COURTESY OF DIPANI SUTARIA

The pesky crows caught a baby squirrel one day, and young Dipani got it away from them. But she didn't know what to do next, and the squirrel didn't survive. "I cried a lot," she remembers, "but then I realized that these things happen in nature and you can't stop them." That was her first lesson in ecology.

"Do what you want to do. There's always a way. If you have an idea or a passion, approach the people who can help you. Don't worry. If you find an organization you like, contact it. Don't hold back. But always be open to sharing and open to criticism."

Seeing her growing love for animals, Dipani's dad started to show her nature programs. He showed her a film about dolphins in captivity that made her upset, and another where a killer whale proved that it could tell a good person from a bad one. The good person was a scientist.

All through her schooling, Dipani dreamed of being in the wild, observing animals, asking questions and using her passion to protect them. After finishing her undergraduate degree, she wrote letters to as many different wildlife researchers as she could find. One replied and invited her to work on sea turtles. She traveled to an island in the Bay of Bengal where she could walk at low tide among crabs and shorebirds, everyone doing their own thing side by side at the water's edge. She helped monitor the thousands of olive ridley turtles that come out of the ocean at the same time to nest on the beach. "It remains my most favorite place on the planet," she says.

While getting to the islands by boat, she saw dolphins in the wild for the first time. "It was a moment of quiet, peaceful awe. A mother and her child were rolling slowly and gently over each other." After circling the boat, they left and Dipani went back to her work, but all she could think about was dolphins.

Dipani's photography skills and knowledge of cetacean behavior have allowed her to take photos like this one of an Indo-Pacific humpbacked dolphin (*Sousa chinensis*). She uses her photos to identify and track individual animals. *DIPANI SUTARIA*

One day she walked the beaches to look for dead turtles and found a dead bottlenose dolphin too. She decided she had to learn more about **cetaceans** (whales, dolphins and porpoises) in India. But the only information she could find was records of dead animals.

"That's when it struck me that we didn't know anything—no one was studying them in India."

She learned how to study dolphins by doing a master's degree in the United States; then she went to Thailand to learn more. There she met other South Asian researchers and learned about Irrawaddy dolphins found in rivers, lagoons and coastal areas of Asia. She found out that India has a small popu-

> **DID YOU KNOW?**
> There are at least 30 different species of cetaceans found in India.

lation of Irrawaddy dolphins that are only found in and near a lagoon called Chilika on the eastern coast. She also learned that many people were taking tourists by boat to see them, but no one was controlling that activity or knew how it might be impacting the dolphins. Dipani imagined how much stress they must have been under, living so close to humans. She felt inspired and decided to study dolphins as a PhD student.

One of the main ways people study whales and dolphins is by taking photographs of individuals. Dipani learned to predict when and where they would surface for a few seconds to get air. She would position herself in a rocking boat, ready to take pictures that would help her tell one dolphin from another and explain where they went and which other dolphins they hung out with.

She found out how many dolphins there were in the lagoon, where they were, how they interacted with each other and what was affecting them, like getting caught in fishing nets and being disturbed by boats. She also talked to local people and found out

Dipani gets to know a fishing family in the state of Gujarat. To do her research, Dipani relies on local fishers to take her out to sea on their boats. It's important for her to understand how her work may affect them.
COURTESY OF DIPANI SUTARIA

that they loved having the dolphins nearby—they didn't want to harm them.

Dipani concluded that the Chilika Lagoon dolphins were at extremely high risk of going extinct, so she sent a recommendation to the International Union for Conservation of Nature to have them listed as critically endangered. She also said that any efforts to protect the dolphins needed to involve local people.

"They say knowledge is power. 'Knowing' consciously brings passionate changes in an individual's life. At home we make our own compost and buy unpackaged food. We have to start the change at home before going out on the streets to make it happen."

Before any wildlife can be protected, people have to care about it. To care, people have to know it exists. Dipani realized that very few people in India knew their country even had cetaceans.

She began to give talks at conferences, film festivals and wherever else she felt she could get the word out. Students came and told her they wanted to do something but their professors were discouraging them from suggesting new projects. She encouraged the students to apply for funding and do the work anyway. She also started training students to do marine mammal fieldwork. I asked her which university was paying her to do that, and she just laughed. She wasn't getting paid.

"There's nobody else yet in India who's doing this," she told me.

Because of Dipani's efforts, more and more Indians are studying marine mammals.

"We had no idea about the populations or diversity of marine mammals in India's waters. I've started a movement where people are starting to care about these things, and we're getting more information. Students finally feel that this is something they can work on, and they don't feel intimidated by the lack of funds or guidance."

One year, one of Dipani's students supported a village south of Mumbai to help a dolphin after it went too far inland and got stuck in a river, separated from its family. Fishers used their boats to nudge it downstream and their nets as barriers to keep it from going upstream. The local government and a local tourism company guided the dolphin with boats and kayaks until it was safely out at sea.

Dipani tells people this story to show that when you want to help animals, you also have to think about the needs and knowledge of local people. And when you do, great things can happen.

"There's a very personal touch," she explains. "You can't do ecological research or bring a stop to harmful events without involving people. Their livelihoods are at stake." Whether you want people to help a stranded animal, change their activities so they don't harm cetaceans, or take you by boat to your research site, you have to think about how it will affect them. "They need to know there's somebody looking out for them too, not just for the dolphins."

When people work together and show that they care about something, it's more likely that the government will care too. India has a huge coastline that faces a lot of pressures—from

Dipani says...

WHAT CAN YOU DO?

"If you live close to the sea, look at your local fish market and ask what kind of fisheries were involved. Are they dolphin-friendly? Ask fishers about their story, their well-being and what they see out at sea.

Write about dolphins in captivity. Do research on why dolphins should not be in captivity. Read about the kinds of fisheries that are fatal to dolphins, and don't eat those fish."

A fisher in the state of Tamil Nadu shows Dipani his catch. Learning what local fishers catch and how helps Dipani be a better scientist and make recommendations that benefit the animals and local people.
COURTESY OF DIPANI SUTARIA

overfishing to pollution to oil and gas exploration. To Dipani, it seems the government considers these activities to be more important than conservation in the ocean. If there were professors teaching students about marine mammals, more films and news stories about those marine mammals, and more people involved in coastal projects, she says, perhaps people would make sure the oceans are healthy enough that people and wildlife can carry on their activities side by side along all the coasts.

DID YOU KNOW?

Irrawaddy dolphins seem to spit water, which makes them look like cartoon characters. They're probably filtering out water and keeping in little fish to eat.

Living Vegan

SAMEER MULDEEN

Executive manager
Born and lives in Montréal, Québec

My mother is Haitian, my father is Guyanese. I was bilingual at home. I consider myself a Montréaler first, which has its own reality different from the rest of Québec and Canada.

"I was the most carnivorous person ever," Sameer Muldeen remembers, with a glint in his eye. "I hated vegetables. Meat was my life. Anytime there was a barbecue, I was cooking the meat. Even today I still think it's probably delicious; however, I just choose not to consume it."

The meat-eating years of Sameer's life were ordinary. He did well in school, got married, had a steady job and bought a house in a suburb. Then he had a bit of a midlife crisis. He'd done everything he was supposed to do—now what? Did he have anything meaningful to give back to society?

An animal cruelty video had been sitting in his email inbox for months. He'd seen videos like that before, but they had

As a mixed child of first-generation parents, Sameer's self-identity changed at different times in his life.
COURTESY OF SAMEER MULDEEN

never had any effect on him. He decided to watch it. At that time in his life, he knew something needed to change, and suddenly that video hit home. Seeing animals being mistreated on fur farms, he realized how his choices about what he was buying were affecting other living creatures. He questioned whether animal products were necessary for our well-being and realized that the power to make a difference was within him.

"I thought, I cannot encourage animal exploitation in any way, shape or form," he recalls. "I decided not to buy any animal product ever again, because the animal likely went through something similar to what I had just seen—only to satisfy our pleasures."

That New Year's Eve, Sameer was offered turkey, but he refused to eat it. After eating just the side dishes, he felt pretty good. He tried living without meat for a few weeks, read more about it and decided to carry it on as a personal experiment. After a few months, he cheated once, with a pork burger, and felt terrible. Physically and emotionally, his body told him there was no going back.

He realized that the majority of livestock must be *factory-farmed* to meet uninformed people's demand for animal products. That kind of farming contributes to *deforestation*, pollutes waterways and is a major source of the greenhouse gases that cause climate change.

> **DID YOU KNOW?**
> Canada's new food guide includes a recommendation for people to eat more vegetables, fruit, whole grains and protein-rich foods, especially plant-based sources of protein.

This would be his cause.

As Sameer changed his diet, people told him he had to eat meat to be healthy. He decided to prove them wrong, to be an example to others. He became fully **vegan**. It was his way of following Mahatma Gandhi's words, to be the change he wanted to see in the world. Some people were inspired by or at least curious about his decision; others rejected it, especially his relatives. Oddly enough, those same relatives eventually asked him for health advice. "I didn't always convince them, but I definitely got their attention."

This inspired Sameer to take things beyond his personal experiment and begin to influence others. He saw two means for making changes. The first was top-down, by getting involved in politics. The second was bottom-up, by leading activities in his community.

Politically, Sameer found that the party with the strongest interest in animal welfare was also the one with the strongest environmental platform—the Green Party of Canada. He decided to join, first as a volunteer and eventually as a candidate for the federal election. He saw that the Green Party's work on animal welfare could be better coordinated, so he tried to pull it all together. The party leader gave him a position as an animal issues critic. Sameer also introduced Georges Laraque, a Haitian Canadian professional hockey player, vegan and animal welfare activist, to the Green Party. Georges ended up becoming deputy leader of the party, generating a lot of media attention.

Sameer says...

WHAT CAN YOU DO?
"Invite a friend to enjoy a vegan meal with you."

Sameer began to notice that it was common for vegans and vegetarians to be environmentally conscious. He also met many environmentalists who were concerned about fossil fuels, waste and air pollution from cars and complained about the actions of big companies, but who didn't want to talk about how their own food choices affected the environment. Sameer found it frustrating.

> "If you want to be an activist playing music, do that. If you want to write blogs, be a lobbyist, organize marches, bake a dish, do research, you name it—everything works and everything is important. Have fun doing it. Then, even if there's no result, the process is worthwhile."

"Environmental issues had their share of attention," he remembers. "But our eating habits and how they affect the environment—very few were talking about that. That was my opportunity to do something different."

Regardless of how people voted politically, they were voting for or against the environment when they chose what to eat. These choices set an example for other consumers and are a powerful yet accessible way to influence the food industry, which supplies things that people want to buy.

Sameer wondered about ways to get people to change their behavior and decisions about what they put into their bodies. "You need a mix of approaches and messages that can say the same thing but in a different way. Eventually you'll reach a wide range of people. To realize any change, you must let a person follow their own path."

Sameer tried a lot of things. He hosted a radio show called *Perspectives véganes*. He became the president of the Montreal Vegetarian Association and was involved in creating Montreal's first Vegan Festival, making sure it was environmentally friendly. In its first year, 4,000 people attended. The year after, 10,000 attended.

Sameer has found that people often choose to be vegan or vegetarian for health, animal welfare and/or environmental reasons. *ANNA_ SHEPULOVA/ISTOCK.COM*

To Sameer, that demonstrated that there's an interest in the way we eat.

His goal was always to help people learn about why and how to try a vegan diet, even part of the time, and how to be healthy and have fun while doing so. Fun has always been an important part of Sameer's work. He found that many other activists got angry while they were working toward big goals, and they'd get bitter if they didn't reach them.

"Guyana and Haiti are Caribbean cultures," he explains. "They're about food, music and enjoying the present moment in a slow-paced lifestyle. We also try to have fun doing everything. We have fun cooking. We have fun dancing. We have

> *"Don't be afraid to take breaks. It's hard to make a change and it's okay to pause, to pass the torch as an activist and to move on. Respect your limits."*

fun arguing. We argue and then laugh about it. I try to have fun whenever I'm doing something, even activism."

Sameer also tries to be patient, especially when things don't work out. Knowing that his parents had close to nothing when they immigrated to Canada helps him appreciate every life gain and how small things can add up to make big changes over time.

> "Be ready to seize an opportunity. If you want to influence politics or the media, prepare your idea in advance, and when the right politician or journalist can carry the issue for you, hand it to them."

Over the 10 years since he began his activism, Sameer has found that more people are becoming vegan, many of them to reduce their contributions to climate change. He's happy to have set the stage for others to carry on his work.

"You look back and say, 'What did you do about the environmental crisis?' I tried to consume better and I tried to influence other people to consume better," Sameer says. "I'm happy that now it's less of a confrontation when you say you're vegan or vegetarian, compared with what it was like 10 years ago. The fact that it's more accepted and there are more vegetarian or vegan options lets me believe that I've done my part."

DID YOU KNOW?

If you want to make environmentally friendly changes to your diet, it doesn't have to be all or nothing. Every action counts.

Animal-welfare and environmental movements often clash. But to Sameer, they're tightly connected because our food choices have corresponding environmental effects. *RESPECT-ANIMAL.CA*

Nitya Chari Harris says we are connected to everything in this universe and that we need to act in ways that honor that connection. *CURTIS ANDREWS*

Coexisting with Carnivores

NITYA CHARI HARRIS

Chair, Coexisting with Carnivores Alliance
Born in Mumbai, India; lives in Langford, British Columbia

*I identify myself by the work I do that makes
me feel that I'm doing my life's purpose.*

Nitya Chari Harris gets her adventurous streak from her dad. When she was young, he took their family camping in national parks throughout Canada and the United States. The vast and beautiful vistas amazed and inspired her. When she was 11 years old, her father took them to Georgian Bay, in Ontario. The pristine water and the lands surrounding it carried an energy that grabbed her and held her. At the time she didn't know it was possible to work with nature, but she kept this inspiration in her back pocket from that moment forward.

Nitya (right) and her family were among the first Indian families to move to the now cosmopolitan Brampton, ON.
COURTESY OF NITYA CHARI HARRIS

The camping trips and immersion in nature represented only a fraction of Nitya's early life. She spent the rest of it in an urban setting. But the dramatic landscapes from those trips stayed with her so much that when she finished her engineering degree she decided she wanted to live near the mountains. She had job offers in Ontario, close to where her family lived, but chose the mountains instead. So she packed up and left for Calgary, Alberta. The first thing she did when she arrived was hop on a bus to Banff, in the Canadian Rockies.

> "When we moved to Canada, I was 11 years old. I was the only Indian child in my class, in my neighborhood. I think about how much I changed myself to fit in. If I had someone tell me that it was okay to just be me and find people who appreciated me for what I was, it would have been better. Be yourself, whoever you are, do whatever interests you, and it will all work out."

To support this fresh start, Nitya needed a job. Everything available in Calgary was in the oil and gas industry, so she became a gas reservoir engineer, then a pipeline engineer. But right from day one, Nitya remembers, "It felt really antagonistic. I didn't feel inspired or creative, or that it was my life's work. It felt like I wasn't fulfilling what I was supposed to be doing."

Nitya was earning easy money, but she wasn't happy. She got out of the city as often as she could, spending her spare time in the mountains, where she really started to develop a connection with nature. As she walked the land, she got an urge to do something more with her life. She still wanted to be an engineer, but in a way that was environmentally positive.

Her unhappiness just kept building as the years wore on. Then she heard about a master's program in environmental design. The more she learned about it, the more it sounded right for her.

Nitya's motivation for doing environmental work comes from the earth, from walking the land and being in nature.
SCOTT STUART HARRIS

She quit her job. Her company was shocked; it was such a big decision, especially since her husband also didn't have a job at the time. But for Nitya the decision felt right. "It felt more in line with who I was. The oil and gas work wasn't for me, and it wasn't good for me either. You've got to really listen to yourself and see if what you're doing makes you happy. I didn't for a long time."

Nitya and her husband traveled to British Columbia one summer, and that was enough to convince them that it was home. So after she finished her degree, they left Calgary and found a house in the woods on Vancouver Island.

"The more time I spent in nature, the more I wanted to do work with nature." The engineering became secondary, and

DID YOU KNOW?
A wolf pack protects and feeds nursing mothers. Sometimes members of the pack babysit pups while their parents are hunting for food.

working directly with the natural world became her focus. "It took me a long time to find the work I'm doing now." Rather than waiting for the perfect job to appear, she let the world be her guide.

One day Nitya was out walking in the forest behind her home and came across a wolf in a trap. "It was a young wolf, less than a year old. Unfortunately, its leg was broken, so it had to be put down. It made me realize how close we live to these large carnivores and how they are affected by our ignorance and our not respecting them."

Soon after, she heard that four cougars—a mother and three babies—were killed nearby because they were eating a goat on a farm. "That confirmed for me that because we are living here, the large carnivores are losing out. Any time there is a conflict, they lose. It's driven by fear, ignorance and apathy. I wanted to find solutions so that we can live here, but they can also safely live in these areas."

Nitya started the Coexisting with Carnivores Alliance, aimed at finding ways for people who live in areas close to the habitat of large carnivores, particularly cougars, wolves and bears, to peacefully coexist with them. The alliance is a large group that includes government representatives, Indigenous and non-Indigenous

---

Nitya says...

WHAT CAN YOU DO?

"Find something small in your own life or close by that needs work, that you're interested in and passionate about, and work on it. You're the best person to address it, because it's right there in your life. Put your effort in, and you'll find that will give you strength and bring others to you, and that will be your thing."

Left: Nitya and her husband are part of a farming cooperative and grow a lot of their own food, like these tasty potatoes. **Right:** Nitya thinks we are part of a big field of energy and that whatever we do causes a ripple in this energy field. *SCOTT STUART HARRIS*

people, scientists, farmers and conservation groups. It's a rare opportunity for different people to talk to each other.

"Around this table," she says, "everybody talks. Everybody gets some positive information, advice or help."

Before she started the alliance, those same people had little reason to speak with each other. "Now I see them trying to find ways to work together, supporting and encouraging each other. It gives me a lot of energy when I see that. I think we'll come up with better solutions, because they're all there."

Sometimes she wonders why she chose to work on bears, cougars and wolves instead of something less charismatic but just as important to the ecosystem—slugs, for example. "I justify to myself that I'm not here to say bears are better than slugs but to help people see that all of these things—bears, slugs, trees, rocks—have value in themselves. Bears and cougars are easier to exemplify because people can relate to them. I'm working on our evolution toward valuing everything on this earth."

Nitya points out that the cultural norm in the West is to place human beings at the peak of what is on earth. Many Eastern cultures and philosophies, on the other hand, see value in everything, as part of the whole earth spirit.

"There are no limits to what you can do. Don't let what you see out there prevent you from going beyond. What's out there is just a starting point. You'll find a way to get past all these limits to ideas, to how we live. You can find solutions that go past all that."

"When we crush any parts of that web by our ignorance," she says, "we're destroying much more than we realize, not only physically but also spiritually."

As Nitya has gotten deeper into her work on carnivores, she has also begun to explore ancient Indian concepts of energy fields from both spiritual and scientific points of view. Indian culture has the concept of pranayama (breath extension or control; prana means life force).

"There were tips and tools that old rishis (sages) learned through meditation and pranayama practices that relate to the feeling that we are part of a whole and that whatever we do is a little ripple that carries through this whole field of energy, affecting everything in some way," Nitya explains.

"The bottom line for me is that this is just one little piece of a big pie. We are connected with everything. Connecting ourselves with large carnivores exemplifies that. Connecting with cougars is hard when we think, 'How can I connect with this creature that can eat me?' It's easy to say they're the 'other' and kill them off. This project is my way to show people that we're connected with everything. How people can help is by finding their own connections with this earth, and honoring this connection."

Nitya founded the Coexisting with Carnivores Alliance to help address how people live with the bears, wolves and cougars with whom they share the land. The group provides solutions to human-animal conflict, education and information on how to protect spaces where carnivores live and grow. *YURY SEVRYUK/ISTOCK.COM*

Six

SHOWING
A BETTER
WAY

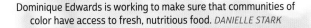

Feeding the Food Desert

DOMINIQUE EDWARDS

Urban planner
Born and lives in Michigan City, Indiana

I'm an African American woman.

At the age of nine, Dominique Edwards knew she wanted to be a scientist—any kind of scientist. She entered her school science fair every year. Sometimes she won awards, like the one for her project on **vermicomposting**, when she was 12.

"I didn't know what it was called at the time," she says. "I just remember I did this really cool project where I got a big pickle jar, put worms and dirt in it, and then took Polaroid pictures of the stages and the tunnels the worms went through."

She remembers going to a friend's house one day as a teenager, and the tap water didn't taste right. "When I went to different places and neighboring cities, I recognized that the water didn't taste the same." In some places it looked funny or tasted strange. "Before I knew it, I was going to different places taking water samples because I wanted to get them tested."

After completing a degree in biology, she moved to Indianapolis to begin a career in the sciences. She started working in a laboratory, but eventually moved back home to Michigan City.

Before Dominique moved to Indianapolis, though, her mother had passed away, as a result of complications from diabetes. Her family had started growing their own food as one way to cope with the trauma of losing her, as well as to address the lack of nutritious food in the community that led to conditions like diabetes.

When Dominique returned to Michigan City, she started her own business making natural products, trying to use plants she could grow and harvest locally. She also got inspired to build a community garden. A national organization was going to help set up the garden, but its budget was cut at the last minute. Then Dominique tried to get people from the city government and from local homeless shelters involved. She advocated for two years, but no one was interested.

Dominique with her dad at her childhood home. Growing food together was therapeutic for their family. *DANIELLE STARK*

Dominique felt rejected by her community. She wanted to leave and never come back. After thinking more about it, though, she wondered if her difficulties in setting up a community garden were just the symptom of a much deeper problem in the way cities were designed. She decided that she needed to go back to school to understand what was happening and what she could do about it. She was accepted to do a master's degree in sustainable urban development and food systems.

"That was right before we started becoming a *food desert*," Dominique says. A food desert, according to the US Department of Agriculture, is an area that doesn't have access to whole foods like fresh fruit and vegetables. This usually happens in impoverished areas that don't have grocery stores or farmers' markets.

"We must organize within our communities to put pressure on political leaders to make sure our people have access to the most basic resources."

Dominique's area of Michigan City didn't have access to enough healthy food to sustain the families who lived there. Her family also lost access to their land and was no longer able to grow food. She learned as well that in different places in the United States, certain industries were often concentrated in and around communities of color. The pollution from those industries put people's health at risk by contaminating their air, soil or water with hazardous chemicals. Dominique saw this *environmental racism* happening where she grew up and near her school.

Sometimes people didn't even know that companies were polluting their communities. Some didn't know that they lived in a food desert. Dominique's own family hadn't realized that the land where they had been growing food was polluted with lead, and the city wasn't planning to do anything about it. Even if

Dominique had been successful in getting a community garden in her neighborhood, she would have had to figure out how to make sure they weren't planting in contaminated soil.

Dominique realized that it wasn't a coincidence that many communities of color lacked different kinds of resources, including access to nutritious food—it was by design.

"Decades of race-based policy-making, racial segregation and slavery have had a negative impact on how our communities are designed," Dominique explains bluntly. "We live in a capitalist society that prioritizes the rich over the poor and puts profit before people. One thing I never considered when I was advocating for community gardens was how policies past and present have designed our cities so that there are marginalized people who are separated from access to food, health care, safe housing and education. Those of us who study things on an economic and social level see it for what it is: the level of white supremacy that's shaped our nation."

While discovering all this, Dominique also started to learn about positive efforts by various organizations, like the Kheprw Institute, which is led by people of color. These organizations were working with communities and youth for racial equality in food systems, and using hydroponics and aquaponics to grow food without soil.

Dominique says...

WHAT CAN YOU DO?

"Get active. Continue your education. Network with your friends, family, teachers and classmates and start a revolution locally around issues in your school or community that will negatively impact you. That's how you get rooted in activism."

For one of her school projects, Dominique used geographic information systems to map out the kinds of food people have access to in northwest Indiana. She mapped public transportation systems, grocery stores that carried fresh produce, farms, uncontaminated vacant lots and population densities. She showed how far people had to travel to get nutritious food, whether they could get there using public transit, and where food hubs, community gardens and urban farms could be set up. Her maps showed that the entire city of Gary was one of 22 communities in northwest Indiana that were food deserts: people had to go to other cities to get fresh produce. She found out that one out of every seven people in the region didn't have access to nutritious food.

It was around this time that the movement in response to violence against African Americans was getting stronger. Seeing case after case of black people being targeted and murdered by police lit a fire under Dominique. "At the height of the Black Lives Matter movement, my interest and drive for community-based

> *"Learn how to be an asset to your community. A lot of people feel there's no value in their community. You have to add value. Be creative, entrepreneurial. You have the ability to contribute positively. If we all jumped up and left, what would we have left to come home to?"*

DID YOU KNOW?

There can be more organisms in a handful of soil than there are people on the whole earth. Healthy soil can contain bacteria, fungi, arthropods, algae, protozoa and nematodes.

---

activism, social justice and Black liberation really took shape. I stayed in the food justice realm and became an expert in local and regional food systems, trying to reshape what they look like."

> *"Never give up. Never be afraid to start over. Never be afraid of failure. One of my mentors told me that the word* fail *is an acronym for* First Attempts In Learning."

People needed to learn about the facts she was uncovering that showed racial inequalities in the food system. Dominique was terrified of public speaking—she didn't think she had the stomach or the voice to do it. What she was learning about was so important, though, that she knew she had to get past her fears. And she's glad she did.

"It made me grow a lot as an individual," she says. "I feel empowered when I'm doing public speaking and there's a diverse crowd. The thing about food is that it connects all of us. I believe that with education comes change."

Dominique started giving talks about food deserts, environmental racism and ways to improve people's access to healthy food. She presented her research at local and regional conferences, at Harvard University and to nonprofit organizations, government

DID YOU KNOW?

If your soil is polluted, you can still grow many fruits and vegetables in containers or raised beds with fresh, clean soil and a barrier at the bottom that separates them from the ground but lets water pass through.

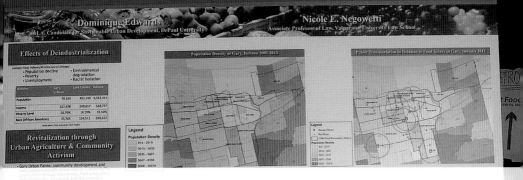

officials and politicians. She also set up a company called Rose and Associates that works on community-based sustainability initiatives.

She had to develop a thick skin to speak in front of some crowds that didn't appreciate her and the fact-based but uncomfortable messages she was presenting. Most times, though, her voice as an educated, articulate woman of color speaking the truth has been an inspiration. Her work was featured in a traveling play that got people to talk about how to revitalize their cities with sustainable food and energy.

Although she didn't fulfill her childhood dream of being a scientist in a laboratory, Dominique is proud of who she is and what she has become.

"My skills and my voice were needed more in my community, and I couldn't do that as a scientist hiding in somebody's lab," she says. "As an activist building community gardens, I ended up becoming an urban planner. That was my goal, to get my master's degree and come back home."

Lucassie Arragutainaq accepts ArcticNet's Inuit Recognition Award for his environmental work. His award was presented at an international conference where Lucassie and others discussed what to do in the face of climate change and other challenges in the Arctic. *COURTESY OF THE ARCTIC EIDER SOCIETY*

Working in Balance

LUCASSIE ARRAGUTAINAQ

Manager, Hunters and Trappers Association
Born in a tent in Upingavialuk (Big Place in the Spring), Nunavut; lives in Sanikiluaq, Nunavut

I'm an Inuk environmentalist.

Lucassie Arragutainaq has lived through not one but three starvations.

"There was one winter inside the igloo when I couldn't go out—I had no clothes. I had to stay inside, naked. I was about three or four years old. There was nothing. I remember my mother making us drink warm water so our stomachs wouldn't have to use energy to make it warm. Nothing to eat. Nothing. Just water. It was really difficult. But we lived through it."

As Lucassie explains this reality, my jaw drops. Then he smiles. "I got to learn to adapt."

Lucassie (bottom, far right) at residential school. He later relearned the value of Inuit knowledge.
COURTESY OF LUCASSIE ARRAGUTAINAQ

Inuit, he says, are very adaptable. They've had to adapt to many things very quickly.

Lucassie was one of 150,000 Indigenous children required by the colonial Canadian government to leave their homes and families to attend church-run residential schools. Residential schools were designed to force Indigenous children—often brutally—to assimilate into non-Indigenous, Christian culture. Students were punished if they practiced their traditions or spoke their Indigenous languages, so Lucassie had to learn English.

> *"Understand who you are and where you came from, and anything is possible. Be responsible. If you try to live differently, it's not going to work. Don't listen to anyone who's not going to help you."*

"When I went to residential school, I thought I was somebody else, not really Inuk," he remembers. But over time he started to accept that he was Inuk, and that wasn't going to change. "That's when I started to think about our cultural values, customs, exactly who I am and where I came from. I started to find out that I had to communicate to the people who they are exactly. Anything is possible."

He also saw that different cultures were unique—but equal. No one culture was better than another, and each had knowledge to share. He started to think about how each one saw the environment and wildlife, and that's when it got confusing.

He gave me a picture of how Inuit see the world:

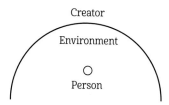

Creator

Environment

Person

"Long before Christianity," he explained, "Inuit would say, 'Someone gave me a polar bear,' or 'Someone gave me a beluga.' They're grateful that they caught it. They won't say, 'I got the polar bear,' or 'I got the beluga.' Respect for the environment and wildlife is very important. Although they kill it and use it, they respect it because if they don't, they'll feel the consequences from the Creator within their lifetime. So they cannot be cruel."

Over several decades, Canada's North and its communities have been endangered by military installations, hazardous waste, mines and huge hydroelectric dams supported by non-Indigenous governments and companies. In looking at how all these activities went ahead, Lucassie saw that the non-Indigenous way of seeing things was opposite to the Inuit's: "The man is on top, the environment and wildlife are small, and that little dot is the Creator. It was really difficult for Inuit people to understand that. How could you be so in control of the wildlife and the environment? I still don't understand it."

Every spring Lucassie and his family go camping near his birthplace. *COURTESY OF LUCASSIE ARRAGUTAINAQ*

More recently, proposed developments have had to go through an environmental assessment process to judge what impacts they might have. But Inuit didn't agree with the environmental assessments done for proposed mining and hydroelectric projects. They didn't match their understanding of the possible impacts. The people proposing and evaluating the projects had a totally different way of understanding the world from that of Inuit, who lived on the land that would be affected. Even their understanding of what the environment was supposed to be like was different from what Inuit knew, because so much had changed already.

"To really understand changes," Lucassie explains, "you have to be there."

In 1997 Lucassie and others pulled together knowledge from Inuit and Cree communities around Hudson Bay to explain their understanding of how the wildlife and environment are supposed to be, and what would happen as a result of one of these proposed projects. They called it Voices from the Bay.

"It's difficult, because in the past we lived sustainably within the environment and with wildlife," Lucassie says. "With all the impacts, we've had to adapt. We're still learning about it, things we never knew before. It's really difficult for us to understand and be part of the environmental assessment process."

DID YOU KNOW?

Lucassie's community of Sanikiluaq relies on the eider duck for warmth and food. This duck has the warmest feathers in the world, which allow it to live in the icy climate and dive into *polynyas*, ocean areas that don't freeze in the winter, to feed on shellfish and sea urchins.

Lucassie (standing) helped the Arctic Eider Society develop an online, interactive environmental monitoring platform called SIKU (the Inuktitut word for "sea ice") for use by people on the land. They worked with Elders and youth to decide which environmental features to include. *COURTESY OF THE ARCTIC EIDER SOCIETY*

As more projects were being proposed in the Arctic, Lucassie went to public hearings—meetings where people who are planning big developments talk to the communities that may be affected. Companies would say they used Traditional Knowledge to do their environmental assessments, but all Lucassie saw in their reports were minor details like locations of tent rings and travel routes. "I thought, 'That's not what I'm looking for.' The information we've gotten from the ends of time can be used—but not in the way they say."

What he'd expected to see was an explanation based on Inuit knowledge about what would happen to the area over time if the development being proposed took place. For example, what would happen if all the toxic waste from a mine went into a lake? How would the company prevent the area from being damaged?

"Nobody knew. They didn't talk about what would happen to the wildlife. They didn't say that any migratory birds that came to that area would be killed. But Inuit knowledge will say that. That's when I decided something needed to be done. There had to be another process."

He noticed that the companies presented the environmental effects as a bunch of numbers. But Inuit, Lucassie says, understand

Lucassie helps Inuit become directly involved in evaluating projects that will affect them, because they are the people with the best understanding of the Arctic environment and wildlife and have the most at stake.
COURTESY OF JOEL HEATH/THE ARCTIC EIDER SOCIETY

the environment and wildlife by their feelings, not by numbers. "People had nothing to say at the public hearings because they didn't really understand what it all meant. But when it comes to wildlife and the environment, everybody wants to participate, because they understand that."

Meanwhile, the companies didn't see how Inuit knew their environment. Inuit are not talkative, Lucassie says. They won't explain everything in detail, like how they go fishing or how they manage wildlife, because they'll assume that if you're an adult you should know these things without having to be told. But the representatives of non-Inuit governments and companies didn't understand without being told, even though they were adults.

Lucassie was afraid that decisions made using numbers alone, without input from Inuit, would hurt the environment. "They don't live in it. They don't eat the wildlife. They don't see the things we care about." He saw that for the companies it was all about economics. Lucassie's community didn't even know what money was 60 years ago—their way of life didn't need it. They've had to adapt to the cash economy too. "In Inuit knowledge, economics is a good thing too, but you have to make a balance. To make a balance, Inuit have to be part of the process."

Lucassie saw that each group of people needed help to understand the other. He's found that persuading companies to do things differently is very difficult. For Traditional Knowledge to be used, it had to be presented in ways that the companies and government already understood. And to ask Inuit to share their knowledge about the possible effects of a proposed development project meant that they had to understand it.

"I tried to learn as much as possible so I could translate for the people. I learned to help our people understand projects so they could be directly involved." Now he's trying to understand the financial side so he can use his tone of voice to translate those numbers into feelings that his community can relate to.

"Somehow, people started listening to what I have to say," Lucassie says. "When people hear me saying something, they understand right away that it might be important. I explain the process that the company or government wants, and ask, 'What's the process we want?' I tell them without ordering them, in a way that they will think about it. Then, if we have something to say, we say it."

In 2017 Lucassie received the Inuit Recognition Award for his work on climate change and environmental issues.

"If we can work in parallel or in balance," he says, "we can work better."

Lucassie says...

WHAT CAN YOU DO?

"Respect other people. Respect the wildlife. Respect the environment. Because those are the only two things we came from: environment and wildlife."

Nancy Huizar combines environmental and social justice work in Seattle. Here she's at a workshop to identify polluted areas and places where Indigenous people are facing barriers to their well-being. *ZORN B TAYLOR*

Bridging the Gap

NANCY HUIZAR

Program manager
**Born and lives in Beacon Hill, Seattle, Washington
(and plans to live there her whole life)**

I'm a Mexican Filipino American, I'm young and queer.

Nancy Huizar's dad used to work on big crabbing boats. The work was difficult and dangerous, but he loved the ocean and passed that love to his kids. Nancy went with her dad to aquariums and watched the movie *Free Willy* over and over and over again. She even saw the actual Willy (an orca named Keiko) and learned about how bad it is for whales to be kept in captivity. Nancy's elementary school in Seattle's South End was next to a forest and a wetland, so her teachers took their classes outside a lot. When she was in first grade, a group called EarthCorps started coming to the school. They led the kids in restoring areas by pulling out invasive plants. Once they got the invasives out of the wetland, the kids could see salamanders.

"It was exciting to see that there were things in there that were kind of cute, to see how we were helping their habitat and not impacting them," Nancy remembers. "It was cool to be a steward of environmental areas."

In fifth grade, Nancy's class read *Hatchet*, a story of survival by Gary Paulsen, and their teacher took them to the forest to see if they could figure out how to survive for a week with only the things they had in their pockets and whatever was around them. All those activities put in Nancy's mind how we can take care of nature, and how nature can provide for us.

Nancy continued to remove invasive plants into her high school years. She also worked at the local science center, taking care of animals and leading nature walks on the beach.

"We grow when we go out of our comfort zone. If you get out of your comfort zone, you'll learn new things about yourself, others and the world. I could tell you what I don't want, but going out of my comfort zone I can tell you what I do want."

The science center had an exhibit on tide pools, but the other staff didn't know how to talk to people about it, especially to kids. Nancy decided to write a guidebook for the staff that explained the animals found in tide pools and how the staff could get people excited about them. Doing that taught her how to talk about science with people in a way that they could understand and have fun.

Nancy's dream was to do research and discover a new species in the ocean. She decided to go to university to study aquatic and fishery sciences.

While studying, she did a research internship with the environmental affairs department of Seattle's public utility company. She surveyed plants around transmission lines and tried to see if hydroelectric dams were affecting fish. What really got her excited, though, was leading the department's outdoor education program with students from an elementary school in South Seattle, where the majority of the kids were not white.

"I took the students to a river where salmon were spawning," she recalls. "They'd never seen salmon in a river before. It was exciting to them. I'm always a fan of getting kids excited about the environment."

Everything Nancy did was fascinating to the kids, even the fact that she was attending university. "There was one little girl who was interacting with me a lot," Nancy remembers. She spoke Spanish, and Nancy responded with the little Spanish she knew. Nancy was proud of what she represented to that girl. "For her to see a woman of color in the environmental field meant she could see herself doing this kind of work."

Nancy received a financial award from her university to do some work within a community. She decided to use it to go back to the same class and develop a lesson plan for them about climate change and its impacts on salmon, the fishing industry and food. "I was really happy to be a part of that, but it challenged me to think about what I wanted to do after graduating. I could do the science thing and be in a research lab, but what if my community isn't going to benefit from the work or understand the impacts of it?"

Nancy also had a hard time finding a job in environmental science after she graduated, even though she already had a lot

DID YOU KNOW?

Nancy's favorite animal is the axolotl, a salamander that is native to Mexico City. It spends all of its time in water. There are very few left in the wild because of poor water quality and loss of the water bodies they live in, but Mexican scientists are trying to bring them back.

Nancy got a job leading projects to restore the vegetation alongside streams to provide habitat and keep the water clean. She directed these volunteers and youth at a creek in Tacoma, WA. *NANCY HUIZAR*

of practical experience. Meanwhile, her white classmates were getting amazing jobs, even when they had little or no experience. But she finally found a job that combined three things she loved: science, restoration and children. She worked with a local municipality, Indigenous people, farmers and volunteers to study and restore water quality in different streams. She went to classrooms and talked to the students about stormwater, where it ends up and the pollution it can carry.

Soon, however, Nancy started to see how her way of thinking was different from that of her colleagues and the organization's directors. "I was the only person of color in the office. After doing a restoration project in a mostly Latino and Black neighborhood and having the contact for the neighborhood be white, I started challenging [my employers]."

Even though she hadn't expected it to be part of her work, Nancy found herself leading a team to train the organization to look at how they could improve racial equality rather than contribute to inequality. "It was very emotional work. I'd be crying."

Nancy's colleagues didn't always appreciate her explanations of how their environmental work was connected to social justice issues. She started to feel uncomfortable, afraid they would belittle her as "the brown girl talking about race again." She wasn't given promotions she felt she deserved, and at times she was asked to train less-qualified people to do advanced jobs that she could have done herself.

> "As hard as it is to be seen, always continue to be seen."

"That was the turning point. I decided to put science down and develop green job pathways for other people of color," Nancy says. "It was hard for me—I felt real emotional pain—but I wanted to make it easier for others later. I got that from my mom—she always tries to make things easier for others. In Filipino and Mexican culture, family and looking out for your own is so important. It hurts me when other people are sad."

Nancy learned about Got Green, an environmental organization led by people of color and people from low-income communities. A survey they did showed that one of the biggest barriers to people pursuing environmental careers was a lack of entry-level jobs. A lot of people couldn't afford to do environmental work

Nancy speaks at a fund-raiser for Got Green to support its work to transform the environmental movement by empowering working-class communities of color. *COURTESY OF NANCY HUIZAR*

as volunteers when they had to support their families, pay bills and put food on the table. Got Green was getting ready to ask the Seattle City Council to pass a resolution to create entry-level environmental jobs for young people of color and other marginalized people. Nancy helped present the case to the council. The resolution passed in 2016.

Nancy is inspired by the motto "Better neighborhoods, same neighbors." While she was growing up in the South End, historically a lower-income area, people who didn't live there tried to tell her it was dangerous and that she had to leave it to be in a better place. But Nancy appreciated her neighborhood and still does.

"It's your family and your community," she says. "Those people saw you grow up and will help you. My mom's whole family moved from the Philippines to our family home, so there's sentimental value. If everyone was told that living in North Seattle is better, then what's left in our communities?"

Nancy has found a way to bring opportunities to her neighbors by working with people who support her values.

"Even if I get knocked down, I keep going. I found a community that has that mentality too. I can't do this work alone."

Nancy says...

WHAT CAN YOU DO?
"Search for groups that fit with your values and what you want to do. Do an information interview: ask people what they do and how they feel. Think about whether you can see yourself there."

Nancy presents information about the challenges of stormwater pollution in Seattle, offering possible solutions.
ZORN B TAYLOR

Finding the Source

WILLIAM PADILLA-BROWN

Farming professional
**Born in Fayetteville, North Carolina;
lives in Asheville, North Carolina**

I'm an African American, Puerto Rican male.

Like many kids, William Padilla-Brown grew up with parents who didn't live together. They lived in different states and sometimes in different countries, so William travelled a lot. His father recruited for the military all over the United States. His mother worked in foreign affairs for the Department of Agriculture, which took her and William to live in places like England, Mexico and Taiwan.

"My mom was always interested in food," William remembers, "and made us try foods in different countries." That woke up his taste buds.

When he was a teenager, his dad took him to his family's town in Puerto Rico. "They had a really cool farm in the forest.

William spent most of his childhood traveling around the world with his mom or dad. When he was older, he took himself around the United States for self-directed education.
COURTESY OF WILLIAM PADILLA-BROWN

William designed his own curriculum, then crowd-funded so that he could travel to classes and events. He wrote papers and made presentations in his hometown about what he learned. *ANTHONY B. RODRIGUEZ*

The houses looked like they'd made them themselves, and there were chickens running around everywhere. I felt connected with it. It seemed mystical, and something I wanted to recreate for myself."

Because he traveled so much, William went to school in a lot of different places, and he started to feel like he wasn't getting what he needed out of the school system. He dropped out at 16 and was afraid he wouldn't get a job. So he decided to create his own education, to create his own job. He started to educate himself with books, documentaries and videos about social sciences, astronomy, biology and the human mind.

DID YOU KNOW?

Every part of a **permaculture** garden plays a role in helping the garden to sustain itself. Some things it can include are vegetables to eat, herbs to deter pests, flowers to attract pollinators and chickens to eat bugs and fertilize the soil.

Around the same time, he decided he was an atheist and left behind his Christian upbringing. Something felt off, though, so he started to study different belief systems and began meditating.

"I realized there was way more to the world than I believed," William says. "I saw a general theme in a lot of the belief systems I studied, which made me want to connect more with a source: my own source, and the source of my food."

He started to research the methods people had used for a long time to grow food. He tried to grow his own food and medicines, and looked for experienced people who could share their knowledge with him.

When he was 18, William ran a nonprofit organization called Community Compassion, which set up gardens in people's yards, harvested the food, shared some with the people who participated and sold the rest at a farmers' market.

William wanted to get closer to where his food came from. This desire took him into the woods, where he learned to identify edible wild foods. *ANTHONY B. RODRIGUEZ*

"As I started to grow food, I realized that everything came from the wild," he recalls. "That had never crossed my mind. That's what got me into the forest. I never went on hikes or camping when I was little, so it was all new."

Then someone told him to check out permaculture. At 19, he took his first permaculture class.

"Permaculture," William explains, "is a whole system design science based on using natural patterns to recreate human systems that are as resilient as natural systems...I was astounded. It exposed me to a world I didn't know about before, but it felt right and was a more sustainable way of living on the land. It got me into learning more about sustainability, *foraging*, *wildcrafting* and farming."

After taking that class, he wanted to learn more, but doing that would mean going to different cities and states for conferences and courses. That would cost money he didn't have. He raised funds for it, though, and treated these studies as if he were going to school. He found mentors in many of the places he visited.

William teaches at the first New Moon Mycology Summit in upstate New York in 2018. The gathering brought people together to talk about earth skills and defense, ecology, permaculture, herbalism and the identification and cultivation of fungi. *HOLLY RAUB/HOLLY WHEAT PHOTOGRAPHY*

William learned how to grow different foods in a permaculture garden and use the carbon dioxide they produced to grow algae that people could eat, make medicines from or use to clean contaminated water. In putting all these things together, he learned how to create a closed-loop system that reused any waste it produced and just created food and oxygen.

He also learned about a lot of opportunities to make people's lives better. For example, if they learned how to pick edible mushrooms from clean, wild areas, people who otherwise had little access to fresh food could improve their nutrition. They could also sell the mushrooms, as William had done to earn income and support his family. He found that being out in nature with others was also fun. Some of his best experiences have been foraging with his friends, making a fire and cooking up whatever they found.

As part of his self-directed schooling, William wrote papers and gave presentations and classes at local yoga studios about what he was learning. He knew that other people in his hometown wouldn't have had any other way to learn about those subjects.

At first, not many people came to his classes. But instead of just bringing him down, that inspired William to do more to make people in his community aware of the benefits of wild plants and mushrooms and increase their environmental literacy.

"Take the time to figure out who you are and what you really want in this world before making life-changing decisions. Stay true to what you find. Stay true to yourself. All of us are unique and all of us have our own gifts to give to the world. Following what you believe in is the best way to give those gifts. Getting to know yourself will lead to success, because you'll always be bringing something that nobody's seen before."

He thought about fun festivals in other places that brought people together around art and nature. He could never go to those festivals because they were far away and expensive to get into. William had recently become a father and couldn't afford to spend his money on anything but his family's immediate needs. "I felt it was important to make something like that available to myself and others who were living in cities and had limited funds."

William started the MycoSymbiotics Mushroom and Arts Festival just outside his city. He invited experts to come and lead nature walks and teach people how to identify edible wild plants and mushrooms. Musicians and artists also came to perform or sell their art. "Every year we get more people interested and out into nature."

After the festival began, he started seeing more people posting on their Facebook pages about wild foods they had found when they were out walking, people who hadn't done those things before. More people started to come out for his nature walks during the rest of the year.

As a kid, William had made rap music but had later stopped. By the third festival, though, music had become part of his life again. He started performing under the name It's Cosmic, composing music about nature, plants, fungi and spirituality.

> **William says...**
>
> ## WHAT CAN YOU DO?
> "Plant a seed and watch it grow. Nurture it, take care of it, and it will take care of you. I wish I'd seen more plants grow when I was little. Be attentive and take care of something that can give you something back, whether it's a flower you can see the beauty of, a bean you can eat or a fruit you can enjoy."

William wished that nature-focused festivals could be more accessible to people with fewer resources who live in cities. So he started his own. *JOANNA MARQUIS*

William has made a name for himself. He's written books about growing edible mushrooms and algae. He travels around the United States to teach courses. He's even been invited to teach at some of those festivals that he couldn't afford to attend. He stands out as a young person of color taking leadership on these topics, so his expertise has caught people's attention.

"I've seen a push in communities to get more people of color involved," he says. "It's beneficial for me and for other ethnic people and young people."

Because of William's background and travels, he feels comfortable in a lot of different social situations. "I often teach in universities or for mushroom clubs. There will usually be a lot of older white people. I'm capable

> "I wish every young person would grow a fruit or a nut tree if they have a place to do it. Then maybe by the time they're my age they'll have fruits or nuts they can use and bring to market."

of communicating with them. I'll teach in Atlanta or Baltimore and there will be younger people, people of color, people from a lower economic status. I'm also capable of communicating with them."

Looking deep within himself has led William to find out how he learns best and to expand his learning outward, especially to people who wouldn't otherwise get the opportunities he sought for himself.

"I feel responsible for sharing this reality that I've experienced with other young people of color," he says. "As I was growing up I didn't know anything about trees or mushrooms, and I know so many people who, without external influence, wouldn't be exposed to these realities for self-growth and the betterment of the planet."

Every year, William's festivals and nature walks get more people interested and out into nature. *ANTHONY B. RODRIGU*

William grows *Cordyceps militaris* fruiting bodies and sells them from his online shop. He also teaches workshops on how to grow this medicinal mushroom. *ANTHONY B. RODRIGUEZ*

GLOSSARY

antiretroviral—a drug used to prevent a retrovirus, such as HIV, from replicating

biodiverse (biologically diverse)—having a variety of living organisms and the ecological complexes of which they are a part; this includes diversity within species, between species and of ecosystems

cetacean—a marine mammal in the order Cetacea that comprises whales, dolphins and porpoises; they have a streamlined hairless body, no hind limbs, a horizontal tail fin and a blowhole on top of their head for breathing

collective—something made, shared or run by everyone in a group

colonization—a process by which a central system of power dominates the surrounding land and people

conservation management—the practice of maintaining a species or habitat in a particular state

contamination—the action or state of making something impure, unclean or polluted, especially by mixing something harmful into it

deforestation—the long-term or permanent loss of forest cover and the conversion of forest to another land use

ecological—relating to or concerned with the relationships of living organisms with one another and with their physical surroundings

ecology—the study of how living things interact with their environment and each other

environmental literacy—the understanding needed, and willingness, to make informed and responsible decisions that consider the well-being of natural systems, communities and future generations

environmental racism—the disproportionate location of polluting industries and other environmental hazards close to racially marginalized communities and the working poor

factory farm—a large industrialized farm, where a large number of livestock are raised indoors in conditions intended to maximize production and minimize cost

food desert—areas of a country, usually impoverished ones, that lack fresh fruit, vegetables and other healthful whole foods, largely because of a lack of grocery stores, farmers' markets and healthy food providers

forage—to obtain something, especially food, from a place by searching

holistic—considering a whole system rather than just its individual components

hydraulic fracturing (fracking)—a process of drilling into the earth and injecting a mixture of water, chemicals and sand at high pressure to force open fissures and extract oil or gas

hydrogeology—the branch of geology concerned with water occurring underground or on the surface of the earth

inclusivity—the practice or policy of including people who might otherwise be excluded or marginalized

indicator—something observed or calculated that is used to show a condition or trend

indigenous—(people) the original inhabitants of a region; (species) originating in and naturally living, growing or occurring in a region or country

invasive plants/species—plants/species that are not native and have negative effects on a region's economy, environment or public health

keystone species—a species on which other species in an ecosystem largely depend, such that if it were removed, the ecosystem would change drastically

mitigation—steps taken to avoid or minimize negative impacts

moratorium—a period of time that is formally agreed on to halt or postpone an activity

mycelium—the mass of fine, branching tubes that make up the part of a fungus involved in growth and nutrition; it can create fruiting bodies, otherwise known as mushrooms, and comes in many sizes, from very tiny to the size of a forest

mycology—the branch of biology concerned with the study of fungi

native plant—a plant that occurs naturally in an ecological region or habitat where over the course of evolutionary time it has adapted to physical conditions and has co-evolved with the other species in the system

old-growth forest—a forest that has trees of all ages, from young to very old, and has never been commercially logged

pastoral—used for the keeping or grazing of livestock such as goats, sheep or cattle

permaculture—the conscious design and maintenance of agriculturally productive systems that have the diversity, stability and resilience of natural ecosystems

polynya—an area of open water surrounded by sea ice

remediation—the process of stopping or reducing pollution that is threatening the health of people or wildlife

renewable energy—energy obtained from the sun, wind, waves or other natural renewable sources, in contrast to energy generated from fossil fuels and other finite sources

restoration ecology—the study and process of assisting the recovery of an ecosystem that has been degraded, damaged or destroyed

sediments—solids, previously suspended in a liquid, that settle at the bottom of the liquid—for example, sand on the sea floor

social justice—equal access to wealth, opportunities and privileges within a society

stewardship—the careful and responsible management of something entrusted to one's care

sustainability—generally refers to the use of resources in a way that maintains ecological balance now and for future generations, although there is no universally accepted definition of the term

Traditional Knowledge—the knowledge, innovations and practices of Indigenous communities, developed from experience over the centuries and adapted to the local culture and environment, although there is no universally accepted definition of the term

unceded—not surrendered; for example, Indigenous Title has been neither surrendered by Indigenous Peoples nor acquired by the federal or provincial government in many parts of Canada's west coast

vegan—using or containing no animal products

vermicomposting—the use of worms to convert organic waste into fertilizer

watershed—a land area that channels rainfall and snowmelt into creeks, streams and rivers, and eventually to outflow points such as reservoirs, bays and the ocean

wayusa—an Amazon rainforest plant used for promoting good health, understanding dreams and uplifting emotions; it is called cushipanga (leaf of joy) in the Indigenous Kichwa language

wildcrafting—gathering herbs, plants and fungi from the wild

RESOURCES

INTRODUCTION

African Centre for a Green Economy: africancentre.org

David Suzuki Foundation: davidsuzuki.org

Marudam Farm School: marudamfarmschool.org

Penashue, Tshaukuesh Elizabeth. *Nitinikiau Innusi: I Keep the Land Alive.* Winnipeg, MB: University of Manitoba Press, 2019.

Students' Sea Turtle Conservation Network: sstcn.org

Sustainable Diversity Network: davidsuzuki.org/take-action/volunteer/sustainable-diversity-network

Tsleil-Waututh Nation: twnation.ca

CHAPTER ONE: GETTING PEOPLE INVOLVED

GATHERING YOUNG VOICES: BRANDON NGUYEN

Toronto Coalition of EcoSchools: torontoce.weebly.com

Toronto Youth Cabinet: thetyc.ca

United Nations Youth Assembly: faf.org

UNLEASH: unleash.org

SPEAKING THE LANGUAGE OF SUSTAINABILITY: NANA FIRMAN

Global Muslim Climate Network: facebook.com/Global-Muslim-Climate-Network-1093227517434837/

GreenFaith: greenfaith.org

Islamic Foundation for Ecology and Environmental Sciences: ifees.org.uk

Timber for Aceh: wwf.panda.org/?20151/Timber-for-Aceh

GETTING YOUR OUTDOOR AFRO ON: RUE MAPP
Healing Hikes: outdoorafro.com/2014/12/we-need-nature-now-more-than-ever/

Outdoor Afro: outdoorafro.com

TREASURE HUNTING: ISMAIL EBRAHIM
Custodians of Rare and Endangered Wildflowers: sanbi.org/biodiversity/building-knowledge/biodiversity-monitoring-assessment/custodians-of-rare-and-endangered-wildflowers-crew-programme

Red List of South African plants: redlist.sanbi.org

CHAPTER TWO: DEFENDING LANDS AND WATERS

PROTECTING ANCIENT RELATIONSHIPS: FLÁVIO SANTI AYUY YÚ
Wayusa School: wayusaschool.com

SAVING GIANTS: KEN WU
Ancient Forest Alliance: ancientforestalliance.org

BC Big Tree Registry: bigtrees.forestry.ubc.ca

Port Renfrew, BC: portrenfrew.com/attractions/

UNITING FOR CLEAN WATER: WILLI NOLAN-CAMPBELL
New Brunswick Anti-Shale Gas Alliance: noshalegasnb.ca

CHAPTER THREE: CLEANING UP THE MESS

SPREADING SPORES: DANIEL REYES
Central Texas Mycological Society: centraltexasmycology.org

Ecology Action: ecology-action.org/circleacres

PREVENTING CANCER: DR. CLOTILDA YAKIMCHUK, CM
Sierra Club Canada: sierraclub.ca

Sydney Tar Ponds Agency: tarpondscleanup.ca

RESTORING ANCESTRAL WATERS: RICHELLE KAHUI-MCCONNELL
How Richelle and the community restored water quality using mussels: hakaimagazine.com/news/maori-mussel-memory

Kaitiakitanga: teara.govt.nz/en/kaitiakitanga-guardianship-and-conservation

CHAPTER FOUR: RESPECTING WISDOM

MAPPING KNOWLEDGE: GHANIMAT AZHDARI
Cenesta (Centre for Sustainable Development and Environment): cenesta.org

Territories and areas conserved by Indigenous Peoples and local communities: iccaconsortium.org

PRESERVING FOREST–PEOPLE RELATIONSHIPS: KENDI BORONA
Gladys Nyasuna-Wanga and Kendi Borona, *Managing Community Projects: TARA and the Abasuba Community Peace Museum* (Trust for African Rock Art, n.d.), africanrockart.org/wp-content/uploads/2013/10/Managing%20 Community%20Projects.pdf

Green Belt Movement: greenbeltmovement.org

Maathai, Wangari. *Unbowed: A Memoir.* New York: Knopf, 2006.
——. *The Challenge for Africa.* New York: Anchor, 2010.
——. *Replenishing the Earth.* New York: Penguin Random House, 2010.

Trust for African Rock Art: africanrockart.org

UNDERSTANDING FISHERIES: SAUL BROWN, 'HAZIL'HBA
Heiltsuk Tribal Council: heiltsuknation.ca

Pacific herring: pacificherring.org

Some Indigenous traditional territories: native-land.ca

National Centre for Truth and Reconciliation: nctr.ca

CHAPTER FIVE: SAVING THE ANIMALS

DISCOVERING DOLPHINS: DIPANI SUTARIA
International Marine Mammal Project, Dolphin Safe Fishing: savedolphins.eii.org/campaigns/dsf

IUCN Red List of Threatened Species: iucnredlist.org

Marine Mammal Research & Conservation Network of India: marinemammals.in

LIVING VEGAN: SAMEER MULDEEN
Montreal Vegan Festival: festivalveganedemontreal.com

Montreal Vegetarian Association: vegemontreal.org

Vegan Outreach: veganoutreach.org

COEXISTING WITH CARNIVORES: NITYA CHARI HARRIS

"Animal Facts: Wolf" (*Canadian Geographic*, 2016): canadiangeographic.ca/kids/animal-facts/wolf.asp

Coexisting with Carnivores Alliance: coexcarnivores.org

Project Coyote: projectcoyote.org

CHAPTER SIX: SHOWING A BETTER WAY

FEEDING THE FOOD DESERT: DOMINIQUE EDWARDS

Black Urban Growers: blackurbangrowers.org

Healthy Food Access Portal: healthyfoodaccess.org

Kheprw Institute: kheprw.org

Miriam Fleming McDonald, Lucassie Arragutainaq, Zack Novalinga (compilers). 1997. *Voices from the Bay: Traditional Ecological Knowledge of Inuit and Cree in the Hudson Bay Bioregion*. Canadian Arctic Resource Committee: Yellowknife

National Black Food and Justice Alliance: blackfoodjustice.org

Rose and Associates: theroseassociates.org

WORKING IN BALANCE: LUCASSIE ARRAGUTAINAQ

Arctic Eider Society: arcticeider.com

Hudson Bay Consortium: hudsonbayconsortium.com

SIKU (the Indigenous knowledge social network): siku.org

BRIDGING THE GAP: NANCY HUIZAR

EarthCorps: earthcorps.org

Got Green: gotgreenseattle.org

FINDING THE SOURCE: WILLIAM PADILLA-BROWN

Fungi for the People: fungiforthepeople.org

Padilla-Brown, William. *Cordyceps Cultivation Handbook*. Self-published, 2016. ——. *Practical Phycology*. Self-published, 2018.

INDEX

Page numbers in **bold** indicate an image caption.

ACKNOWLEDGMENTS

This book would not have been possible without the support and ideas of so many. Thank you to the following:

My family for giving me the space and time to do interviews and write.

The individuals featured in this book for agreeing to participate and for sharing their time, stories, photos and wisdom.

The Access Copyright Foundation, whose grants provided me with the resources to pull together a book proposal, conduct the interviews and write the stories.

The supportive staff of the Saskatchewan Arts Board who guided me through that grant process.

Betsy Warland's Vancouver Manuscript Intensive and my mentor, Rachel Rose, who helped me convert my completely disorganized jumble of thoughts into a book pitch and plan of action.

Robin Stevenson, who suggested I approach Orca Book Publishers with my book idea.

Orca for having faith in me and my idea; Sarah Harvey for her skills and positive attitude; and Kirstie Hudson, Rachel Page, Jen Cameron, Ruth Linka and all the other staff who helped convert it from a Word doc into a real book out in the world. Thank goodness I'm not doing this alone!

Everyone who informed me of or introduced me to someone I interviewed, and people who provided ideas even if I couldn't include them: Andrea Vásquez Fernández, Anthena Gore, Asma Mahdi, Aurelia Kinslow, Camille Fouillard, Caroline

Konstant, Curtis Andrews, David Suzuki, Dina El Dessouky, Donna Miscolta, Elizabeth May, Faisal Moola, Fiona Teng, Janina Budi, Jennifer Deol, Jenny Ambrose, Jodi Stark, Joel Heath, John C. Robinson, Kate Emmings, Kathy Brown, Kyle Empringham, Linda González, Linda Mueller, Lisa Gray, Mark Wilson, Melany Sanchez, Rabz Lanisquot, Rosana Cruz, Sam Ralston-Paton, Sharlene Shaikh, Sharline Chiang, Shayda Vance, Stephan Hoch, Tia Taurere-Clearsky, Vanessa Richards, Ximena Izquierdo Ugaz and anyone else I may have missed.

Everyone whose face lit up when I told them what I was writing about.

My fellow writers in the VONA (Voices of Our Nations Arts) community of writers of color, for their boundless ideas, enthusiasm and willingness to share when I asked for help.

Dr. Mao Angua Amis, Kim Sander Wright and Dr. Ingrid Waldron for contributing to my early ideas.

Nitya Chari Harris for agreeing to be my guinea pig as I figured out my interview questions and story format, and needed a sample story to send around, revise and revise again (and again).

Winnie Hwo and the David Suzuki Foundation's Sustainable Diversity Network, working in parallel to build connections and increase the understanding of how diverse this movement really is.

Deanna Bayne, Kester Reid and April Liu for invaluable support as liaisons.

My longtime inspiration, friend and Elder, Dr. Tshaukuesh Elizabeth Penashue, who has worked tirelessly for decades to preserve her Innu heritage and the beautiful lands and waters of Nitassinan.

You. This book is a dream come true, and I'm grateful that it's in your hands.

CURTIS ANDREWS

ANURADHA RAO is a conservation biologist, writer and facilitator born and raised in the traditional territories of the Anishinabewaki, Attiwonderonk and Haudenosaunee Nations and currently based in unceded xʷməθkʷəy̓əm, Skwxwú7mesh and səlilwətaɬ territories. She has worked on research, conservation, restoration, planning and stewardship projects with communities and organizations on the coasts of Canada and in 12 other countries.

Her worldview and approach to science are heavily influenced by teachings from her Hindu culture and from Indigenous knowledge holders. These teachings and the principles of ecology have shown her that everything and everyone is connected, and that we must remember this in our actions and interactions. Anu finds her happy place when she walks off a beach and snorkels among the creatures of the sea.